2013
UNCORKED!

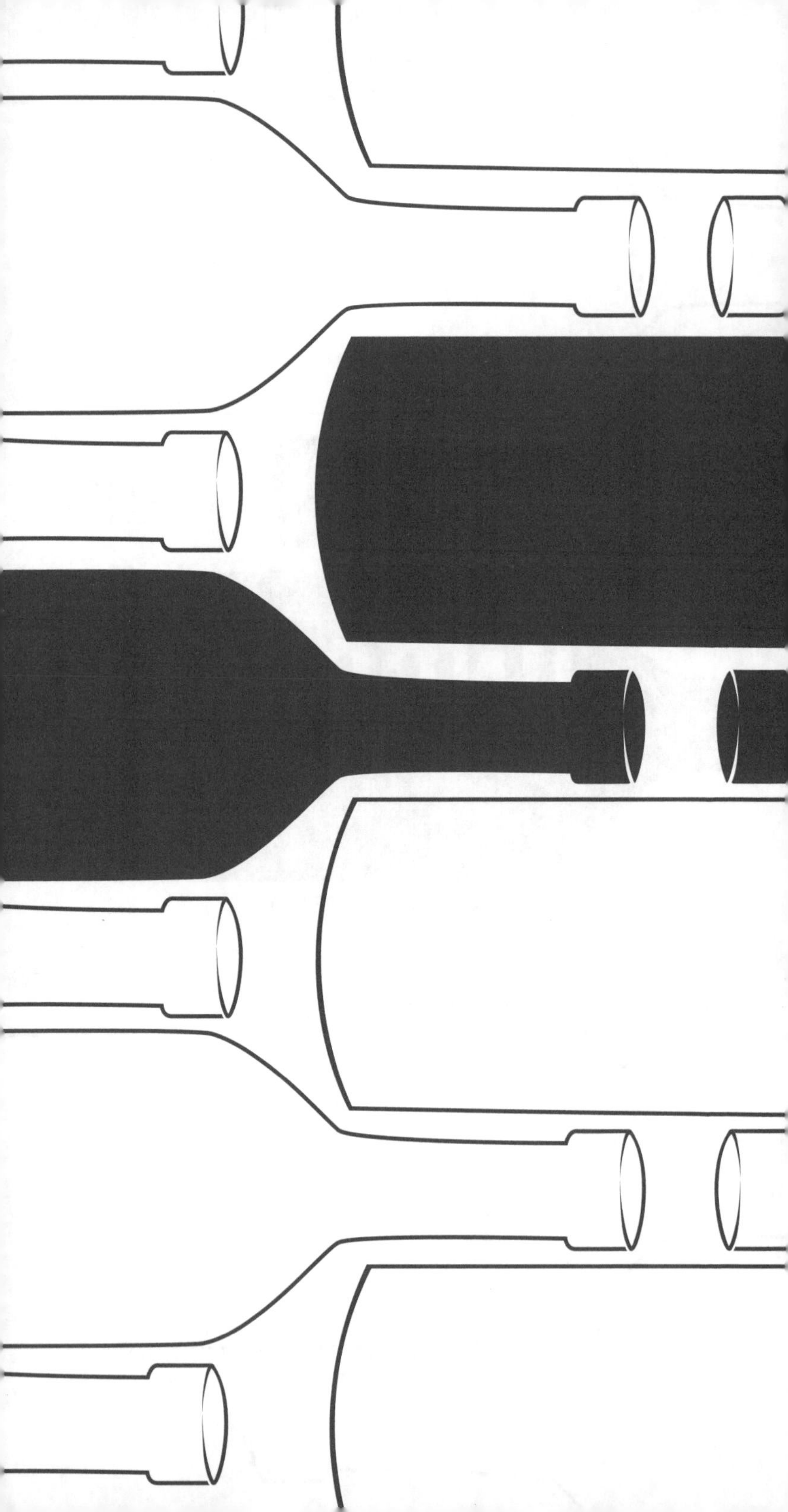

SHELLEY BOETTCHER

2013

UNCORKED!

The Definitive Guide to Alberta's Best Wines under $25

whitecap

Whitecap Books, a Fitzhenry & Whiteside company

Publisher: Michael Burch
Edited by: Carolyn Stewart and Theresa Best
Design by: Setareh Ashrafologhalai
Typesetting by: Michelle Furbacher

Many of the wine label images were provided by wineries and distributors and are reprinted with permission. Others were photographed by the author.

Printed in Canada

Library and Archives Canada Cataloguing in Publication
Boettcher, Shelley, 1970-
Uncorked! : 2013 edition / Shelley Boettcher.

Includes index.
ISBN 978-1-77050-070-9

1. Wine and wine making. 2. Wine and wine making--Alberta. I. Title.

TP548.B63 2012   641.2'2   C2011-908320-5

The publisher acknowledges the financial support of the Government of Canada through the Canada Book Fund (CBF) and the Province of British Columbia through the Book Publishing Tax Credit.

12 13 14 15 16 5 4 3 2 1

CONTENTS

INTRODUCTION

You're holding in your hands a guide to buying 150 wines that each cost $25 or less, plus suggestions for wine and food pairings and more.

If you didn't already know it, this is the second edition of this book. The first—a Canadian bestseller—was released in 2010 and featured great bargains for wine lovers, available across the province of Alberta.

The second book also features fine bargains for wine lovers, available across the province. But a lot has changed in two years, since the first book was released. Vintages have changed, and prices, too. You'll recognize a few familiar labels but, alas, some of the previous edition's picks are now priced too high to be included. Others, for various reasons, just didn't quite make the cut this year.

But—luckily for us—there are a lot of excellent new wines available in the province, new labels that weren't for sale here in previous years.

I have chosen every wine with a metric tonne of care and attention. While importers sometimes supplied wines for consideration, I don't get paid by agents for writing about their wines. Not here. Not ever. As for tasting, I mostly tasted the wines independently, in big blocks of like wines—for example, 10 or 12 Merlot wines or a dozen Sauvignon Blancs at a time. Not every wine tasted ended up in the book. Rather, I took careful notes, and then I chose the best, whittling down the lengthy list of impressive wines for sale in our market. In particular, I looked for top-notch value-priced wines that represent a range of regions, countries, styles and grapes.

Keep in mind that vintages will change as stock sells out at certain stores, but don't worry if you find a different vintage of the same wine; while wines certainly vary from year to year, most of these producers are consistently reliable every vintage.

And although I verified all prices at press time, they may not always be exact. Alberta's liquor market is privatized, which means retailers don't have to charge the same at every store. A $22 bottle at one store may be $17 or, for that matter, $28 at another; shop around and compare.

Still, you get the idea. This book is loaded with 150 fine wines at bargain prices. Buy a bottle or two or 10. Buy a case or two or 10. Taste your way through the world's wine regions, bargain by bargain. Cheers!

—Shelley

HOW TO USE THIS BOOK

How should you read this book? Read it from start to finish, if that's your style. If you know you're a wine geek, pick and choose, based on your favourite grapes, regions or producers. Browse by price. Explore the wine-producing world, country by country or grape by grape. Choose wines for a certain occasion, casual Fridays, Grandma's birthday, New Year's Eve or a family barbecue—I've listed suggestions for each wine under the "Uncork" heading. Or you can just admire the lovely labels.

Each wine listing has this information at the top:

- A listing title (the big, bold text at the top left of each page): Usually this is the name of the wine, but some wines have no particular name; in these cases, I've listed the wine by the most prominent words on the label, to help you find the wine as easily as possible in the store.
- Winery: The company that makes the wine.
- Wine name: The moniker that sets this wine apart from other wines made by the same winery or, for that matter, by anyone else.
- Variety or Type: In the first part of the book (the red wine, white wine and rosé sections), "Variety" is the type of grapes used to make the wine—for example, Cabernet Sauvignon, Sauvignon Blanc, Pinot Noir. In the second part of the book (Bargain Bubbles and Sweet & Fortified Wines), "Type" is the style of wine—for example, Prosecco (a sparkling wine made in Italy), cava (a sparkling wine made in Spain), port (a sweet wine made in Portugal).
- Year: This date—usually called the "vintage"—is the year the wine was made and put in the bottle. A non-vintage (NV) wine is a blend of wines made in different years.
- Origin: The place the wine comes from. This may include the appellation and/or region, terms designated by law to indicate where a wine is made.
- Price: The cost of the wine. I bet you figured that part out by yourself.

I've also made a note of the kind of closure that the wine has, as a point of interest. These are depicted by the following icons:

 Cork (plastic and/or natural cork)

 Champagne/Sparkling wine cork

 Screw-cap closure

 Flip-top trigger closure

TEN TIPS ON CELLARING YOUR WINE

1. **Keep wine out of the kitchen (unless you're opening it).** Corkscrews? Yes. Wine? No. Your kitchen is probably too warm. It's not the best place in which to store wine properly.

2. **Store your wine in the coolest part of your house.** Under the spare-bedroom bed or in a spare closet will work if you don't have a basement, or room for a wine fridge.

3. **Garages are for cars, not cuvées.** Unless your garage is heated, it's too cold in the winter. You'll freeze everything. And your wine can pick up icky smells like car exhaust or mice or just plain ol' dust. Your garage is for empties—until you ship 'em off to a grateful Boy Scout or cash 'em in for money to buy a few new vintages.

4. **Tip 'em over. Gently.** They're not bowling pins. Lay your bottles gently on their sides so their corks touch the wine at all times. (Not a big deal if you mostly have screw caps.)

5. **Turn off the lights.** Keep the room dark. Too much light will fade your pretty labels and oxidize the wines.

6. **Stay away from the cat box, the dog bed, mothballs and oil paints.** Strong smells will seep into your wines. Cat pee may be a desirable odour in some Sauvignon Blanc wines (I'm serious), but let the winemaker decide that. Not you. Or your cat.

7. **Jiggle elsewhere.** Above your washing machine? Or beside your treadmill? Not good. The vibration can damage the corks.

8. **Get wet.** Humidity keeps corks from drying out, and in the cold, dry climate of Alberta, that's important. If you can't afford a humidifier, put a bucket or two of water in your "cellar." The moisture will help maintain good humidity.

9. **Planning to buy a wine fridge? Consider size and noise.** How many bottles do you plan to keep at one time? Does the unit have racks that will fit whatever it is that you prefer to drink? How loud is it when it runs?

10. **Money's no object? Then shop.** Hire a professional. Myriad companies out there will build professional cellars with humidity and temperature controls. Shop around. Ask friends and restaurant staff. Google.

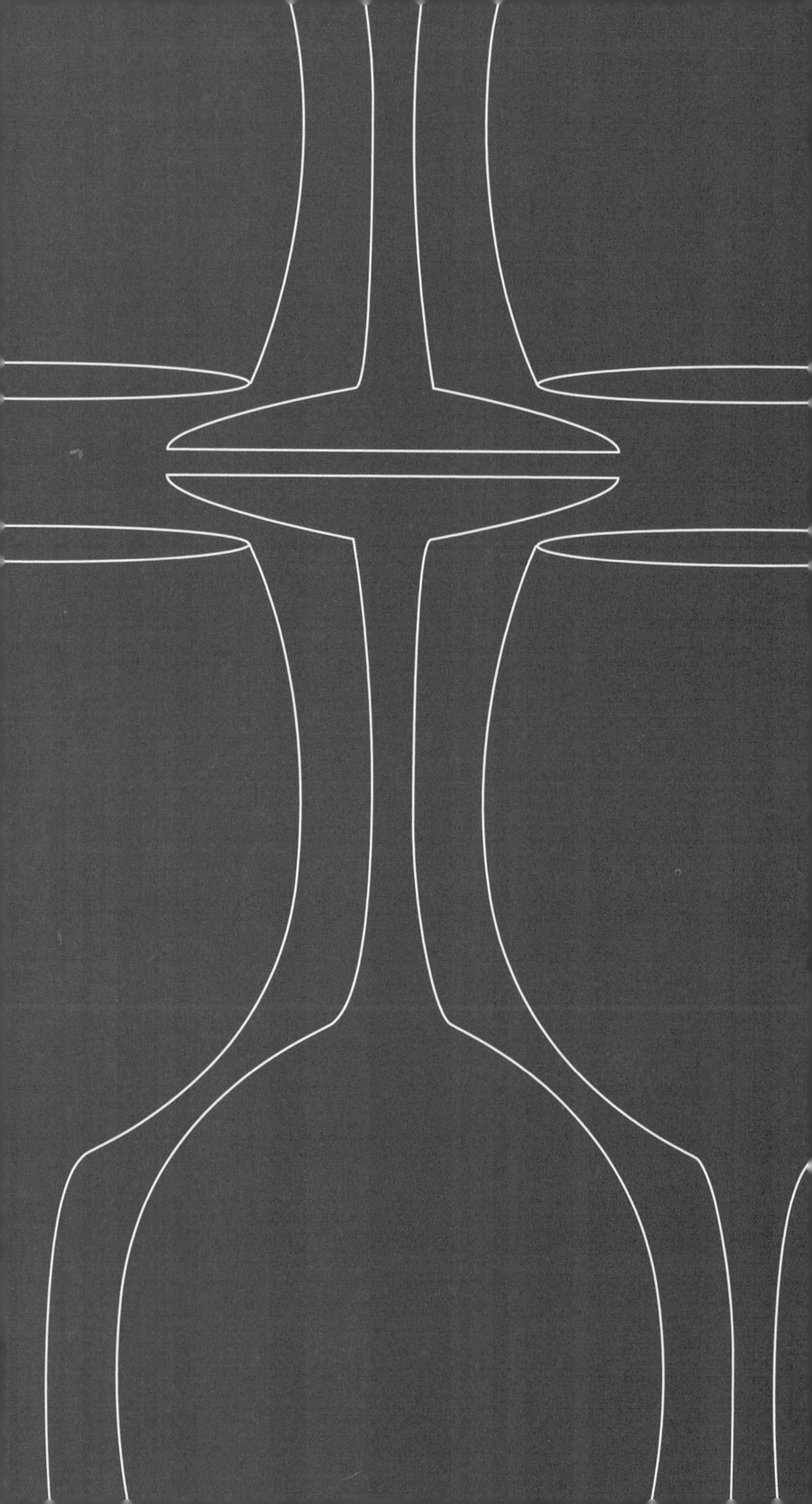

FIRST, THE RED WINES

AMALAYA

Bodega Colomé	Amalaya	
WINERY	WINE NAME	
Organic red blend (see below)	2010	
VARIETY	YEAR	
Valle Calchaqui, Salta, Argentina	$20	
ORIGIN	PRICE	CLOSURE

Amalaya means "hoping for a miracle," which is how I feel when winter just doesn't want to end. The grapes used to make this fruity crowd-pleaser come from some of the world's oldest vines. They date back more than 100 years, and all are farmed biodynamically, without any pesticides and chemical fertilizers.

This blend—mostly Malbec, but with some Cabernet Sauvignon, Syrah and Tannat—is loaded with cherry, raspberry, spicy white pepper notes and a hint of vanilla. Soft tannins, easy drinking.

TRIVIA Salta, Argentina, is home to *el tren a las nubes*, which in English more or less means "the train to the clouds." The third-highest railway in the world, it features 29 bridges, 21 tunnels and two spirals. There is only one spiral on the Amalaya label.

PAIR WITH Steak, roast chicken, roasted Mediterranean-style vegetables, hard cheeses. Very food friendly. Also delicious by itself.

UNCORK Saturday dinners with friends, with graphic designers (who will appreciate the intense blue label), Earth Day, cold winter nights, any time you're hoping for a miracle.

FINCA LOS PRIMOS

Valentín Bianchi	Finca Los Primos	
WINERY	WINE NAME	
Malbec	2012	
VARIETY	YEAR	
Mendoza, Argentina	$13	
ORIGIN	PRICE	CLOSURE

This wine appeared in the 2010 edition of *Uncorked!* Sometimes you just want a red wine that's easy to find, goes with lots of hearty meat dishes and can also be enjoyed just by itself. Here is that wine. Well, here is another one. (I admit I have a few that might fit in that category in this book.) Valentín Bianchi is an Italian who moved to Argentina and started a winery. The name San Rafael on the label refers to a city in Mendoza, the heart of Argentina's wine industry.

TRIVIA In South America, a *finca* is a ranch, a large chunk of rural property.

PAIR WITH Steak, lamb, burgers, ribs. Or drink by itself.

UNCORK Now, at dinner with the in-laws, when you have to bring a red wine but no one told you what's on the menu. Or cellar for up to five years.

TRAPICHE

Trapiche	Reserve	
WINERY	WINE NAME	
Malbec	2010	
VARIETY	YEAR	
Mendoza, Argentina	$15	
ORIGIN	PRICE	CLOSURE

Pronounced *Tra-PEESCH-ay*, this winery was founded in 1883 and is Argentina's largest wine producer. These days, it's owned by a bank, but despite the corporate connection, it's still making some tasty wines, such as this classic Argentine Malbec. Malbec is particularly renowned for making inky, dark wines—such as this one—with plenty of ripe fruit flavours and tannic structure. Just the sort of wine you need on a cold winter night or during a summer barbecue.

TRIVIA The front label features a condor (condors will chase away birds that eat grapes). The sight of a condor would probably chase me away—the world's largest flying bird, it can have a wingspan of 9 feet (3 metres).

PAIR WITH Roast beast (condor may be a bit stringy), hard cheese, steak with chimichurri sauce, stewy dishes.

UNCORK Bank holidays, barbecues, watching hockey games and soccer on TV.

CHURCH BLOCK

Wirra Wirra Vineyards	Church Block	
WINERY	WINE NAME	
Cabernet Sauvignon/Shiraz/Merlot	2010	
VARIETY	YEAR	
McLaren Vale, Australia	$20	
ORIGIN	PRICE	CLOSURE

Wirra Wirra is an Australian aboriginal term meaning "among the gum trees," and this particular Wirra Wirra wine gets its name from a tiny old church located next to the vineyard where the grapes used to make the wine are grown. The first vintage of Church Block was made 40 years ago, in 1972. It quickly became a favourite in Australia and, shortly after that, found fans around the world. A very quaffable, food-friendly red, it has savoury notes of stewed plums, licorice, cedar and leather.

TRIVIA Wirra Wirra is home to the Angelus Bell, a three-quarter-tonne bell that came from a Jesuit church in South Australia but was moved to the winery and restored after the winery owners found it in a scrapyard.

PAIR WITH Meaty dishes, pizza, cheesy crackers.

UNCORK Sunday dinners; any time someone says, "Bring a red," but doesn't tell you what they're making.

FAITH

St Hallett	Faith	
WINERY	WINE NAME	
Shiraz	2009	
VARIETY	YEAR	
Barossa Valley, Australia	$23	
ORIGIN	PRICE	CLOSURE

This wine appeared in the 2010 edition of *Uncorked!* Here's a wine for anyone who needs faith, whether it's believing in something, in someone or simply in the power of a rich, big, powerful red wine. This is a wine for anyone who loves Australian Shiraz at its finest—juicy and jammy, with hints of blackberry and cherries. The winery is named after a long-ago Australian surveyor. As for the "saint" part of his name? No one knows.

TRIVIA We know Shiraz as wine (and a grape). Hafiz of Shiraz was a 14th-century Sufi poet who wrote about love, faith and drinking too much wine.

PAIR WITH Sausages, steak. Or just enjoy by itself.

UNCORK Family gatherings; any time someone says, "Bring a red," but doesn't tell you what they're making.

LAYERS RED

Peter Lehmann	Layers Red	
WINERY	WINE NAME	
Red blend (see below)	2009	
VARIETY	YEAR	
Barossa Valley, Australia	$18	
ORIGIN	PRICE	CLOSURE

This wine appeared in the 2010 edition of *Uncorked!* Peter Lehmann is a real person, an Australian winemaker who's now in his eighties. The son of a Lutheran minister, he considered following his father into the ministry. But in 1945 his dad died suddenly at the age of 55 and, shortly after that, Lehmann dropped out of school to apprentice at a winery. He worked for a while at a distillery and a cooperage before finding his way back to wine. The rest, as the expression goes, is history. This easy-drinking blend is made of five grapes—Shiraz, Grenache, Mourvèdre, Carignan and Tempranillo.

TRIVIA If you play poker (and even if you don't), check out the black clubs symbol on the screwcap; it stands for the gamble that Lehmann took when he started his winery (and helped out some grape-growing friends) many years ago, at a time when people weren't as enamoured with Australian wines as they are now.

PAIR WITH Tomatoey pastas, lamb, stew, burgers, roast chicken.

UNCORK Big family gatherings, rowdy parties, poker night; any time someone says, "Bring a red," but doesn't tell you what they're making.

THE MUSICIAN

Majella Wines	The Musician	
WINERY	WINE NAME	
Cabernet Sauvignon/Shiraz	2009	
VARIETY	YEAR	
Coonawarra, South Australia	$20	
ORIGIN	PRICE	CLOSURE

I love Coonawarra. It feels a bit like Saskatchewan to me—hot and dry in the summer, grasshoppers and tumbleweeds blowing across the road in front of me. And very, very friendly, laid-back people. Alas, Saskatchewan doesn't have those incredible Coonawarra vineyards, such as the ones used to make this rich red, named in honour of a musician friend. The family behind Majella grew and sold grapes for other wineries for many years before deciding to make their own wines. The results are impressive, as this mighty but well-balanced red proves. Soft tannins, lots of Cab and Shiraz flavours, and a smidge of vanilla.

TRIVIA Coonawarra is 27 kilometres long and 2 kilometres wide; within that wee space, there are more than 30 wineries.

PAIR WITH Beef, barbecue, hamburgers, grilled vegetables.

UNCORK During jam sessions, after concerts and outdoor music festivals.

19 CRIMES

Treasury Wine Estates	19 Crimes	
WINERY	WINE NAME	
Shiraz/Durif	2011	
VARIETY	YEAR	
Victoria, Australia	$20	
ORIGIN	PRICE	CLOSURE

Almost 300 years ago in England, if you committed any one of 19 crimes—theft, murder, you name it—you'd be sent to Australia. Back then, the Land Down Under wasn't quite the happenin' place it is now. No good wine. No good rock bands. Not exactly a cutting-edge food scene. Still, people carved out their lives and, along the way, created a country with a colourful history and some of the world's great wines.

Flash forward to the 21st century, and here's a cheeky homage to those long-ago bad boys. This red blend—Shiraz and Durif—is big and bold, with notes of vanilla, licorice and blackberries. Excuse my lame joke, but it would be criminal to gulp this wine as soon as you open it. Decant it or let it sit for a half-hour or so before serving.

TRIVIA The 19 Crimes labels—a series of three—feature black-and-white photos of convicted criminals sent to Australia nearly three centuries ago. Check them out and see if you recognize anyone.

PAIR WITH Burgers, steak, anything big and meaty.

UNCORK Any time you're feeling like a badass. In other words, if you're thinking of buying a Harley Davidson or trying to figure out how to explain your tattoo to your mom.

THOMAS HYLAND

Penfolds	Thomas Hyland	
WINERY	WINE NAME	
Cabernet Sauvignon	2011	
VARIETY	YEAR	
South Australia	$23	
ORIGIN	PRICE	CLOSURE

One of Australia's most famous wineries, Penfolds is known among hardcore wine lovers for its Grange—a big, complex red wine that ages beautifully and, well, costs a lot. Thomas Hyland is considerably more affordable, but still gives a taste of the Grange glamour, with its intense, dark fruit notes and a hint of mint, mocha and spice. And it still comes from the famous Penfolds winery, a pristine property located in Adelaide, Australia.

TRIVIA Penfolds' chief winemaker, Peter Gago, has myriad celebrity friends and fans, including Tool frontman Maynard James Keenan, Diana Krall and Elvis Costello, and Lance Armstrong.

PAIR WITH A perfectly cooked, medium-rare steak.

UNCORK Now, with good friends. Decant it before serving, or at least open it and let it rest for half an hour before serving. Or cellar for up to a few years.

TIC TOK

Robert Oatley Vineyards	James Oatley Tic Tok	
WINERY	WINE NAME	
Cabernet Sauvignon	2009	
VARIETY	YEAR	
Western Australia	$19	
ORIGIN	PRICE	CLOSURE

James Oatley is dead. Love live James Oatley—well, the wines named after him anyway. Oatley was a British convict, banished to Australia in the 1700s. But he turned his life around and became an outstanding citizen and one of the country's top clockmakers. This wine, created by his great-great-grandson, Robert Oatley, is a tribute to him. Get it? Tic Tok.

Before making his foray into wine, Bob Oatley was a coffee- and cocoa-bean marketer. He created Rosemount wines in the late 1960s. He sold the winery in 2001, but not before it had become the second-most-popular Australian winery in the US.

Robert Oatley Vineyards is his new project, and this bold red is part of it. Look for soft tannins, a hint of herbs and lots of dark fruit.

TRIVIA The stylized arrow on all Robert Oatley wines is in remembrance of the symbol—which stood for government-owned property—stamped on the uniforms of all Australian convicts in the 18th and 19th centuries.

PAIR WITH Lamb, hard aged cheddar, steak, hamburgers, bison burgers.

UNCORK Friday night gatherings, NHL playoffs (open it at overtime), Aussie wine fan club nights, any time someone tells you to "just bring a red."

WONDERWALL

Wonderwall
WINERY

Shiraz — VARIETY
2010 — YEAR

Margaret River, Australia — ORIGIN
$19 — PRICE
CLOSURE

According to my various, mostly reliable Internet sources, "wonderwall" is slang for the object of one's affections. Take this wine, for instance. It comes from Margaret River, one of Australia's most beautiful places—in a country that's chock full of beautiful places. You can surf, hang out with kangaroos, wander through wilderness or enjoy incredible cuisine. (Great coffee culture, too. I like.)

Wonderwall is a small winery with a hotshot young winemaker—Jodie Opie. She is involved in many interesting wine projects in and around the region, and she is one winemaker to keep an eye on. However, if you're expecting this to be an overpowering jam bomb of a Shiraz, think again. It's nicely balanced—not jammy, not green—with beautiful fresh pepper and berry notes.

TRIVIA Kids born in 1996, the year that English rock band Oasis had a hit with the song "Wonderwall," will be old enough to drink in Alberta in 2013.

PAIR WITH Hard cheese, meaty dishes. Or just enjoy by itself.

UNCORK With your own "wonderwall," of course!

MIOLO

Miolo Family Vineyards	Reserva	
WINERY	WINE NAME	
Tannat	2010	
VARIETY	YEAR	
Fronteira Campanha, Brazil	$19	
ORIGIN	PRICE	CLOSURE

If you think of Brazil, you likely think of beaches, bikinis, supermodels, soccer and maybe coffee. Not wine.

But winemaking in Brazil dates back to the 1500s, when Portuguese immigrants brought their vines to the country, followed by Italian immigrants in the 1800s. That's how the Miolo winery had its start: the family's ancestors moved from Italy in 1897. For almost 100 years, however, all the family did was grow grapes and make their own wine, until 1992, when they decided to form a winery. Now they make a massive range of wines, including whites and sparklers.

As for this one, it's earthy and intense. Originally from France, the Tannat grape makes dense, savoury, tannic reds that will appeal to anyone who's looking for an alternative to, say, Cabernet Sauvignon.

TRIVIA There are more than 1,100 wineries in Brazil, the southern hemisphere's fifth-largest wine producer.

PAIR WITH Steak, hearty meat dishes, hard aged cheddar. Decant for half an hour to an hour before serving.

UNCORK While watching World Cup soccer games, barbecue nights, dinner with wine geeks.

BLUE MOUNTAIN

Blue Mountain Vineyard and Cellars
WINERY

Gamay Noir	2010	
VARIETY	YEAR	
Okanagan Valley, BC, Canada	$25	
ORIGIN	PRICE	CLOSURE

This wine appeared in the 2010 edition of *Uncorked!* Located near the small town of Okanagan Falls—known by the locals as OK Falls—Blue Mountain is owned by the Mavety family, who started their wine journey by growing grapes for other people, before setting up their own gig in 1991. These days, they're expanding their Gamay production—good news for those of us who like this fruity, lighter-style red wine.

TRIVIA Gamay Noir is an ancient grape used in making Beaujolais wines in France. The earliest recorded mention of it dates back to the 1300s. In France, that is—not the Okanagan.

PAIR WITH Roast chicken, turkey, veal, ham, salmon.

UNCORK Christmas Day, Canada Day, Sunday dinner with friends and family.

CELLAR HAND

Black Hills Estate Winery	Cellar Hand Punch Down Red	
WINERY	WINE NAME	
Syrah/Merlot/Cabernet Sauvignon	2011	
VARIETY	YEAR	
Okanagan Valley, BC, Canada	$25	
ORIGIN	PRICE	CLOSURE

One of the Okanagan Valley's best-known wineries, Black Hills started under the radar, with a cult following that would eagerly snap up its releases—especially the Bordeaux-style blend, Nota Bene—in days, sometimes minutes. That hasn't changed much as the winery has become better known, even after a new winemaker—Graham Pierce—was hired to replace the original co-owner/winemaker Senka Tennant. In response to customer demand, the winery is, for the first time, releasing entry-level-value red and white wines, both priced at $25 or under in BC and Alberta. Actor Jason Priestley is one of the owners; I predict this smooth but intense, dark red blend will bring the folks behind Black Hills even more fame and fortune.

TRIVIA A cellar hand is a person who helps out a winemaker, doing a lot of the grotty and often-boring chores that are part of making wine. To "punch down" means to push the grape skins into the fermenting wine, giving the wine better colour and flavour.

PAIR WITH Grilled meats, vegetables, pizza, lasagna, burgers, you name it. A very food-friendly red.

UNCORK Casual Fridays, Hollywood trivia nights, *Beverly Hills 90210* rerun-viewing sessions. Take a gulp every time you see Brandon Walsh—Priestley's character in the show.

G. MARQUIS

G. Marquis Vineyards	The Silver Line	
WINERY	WINE NAME	
Pinot Noir	2011	
VARIETY	YEAR	
Niagara-on-the-Lake, Canada	$20	
ORIGIN	PRICE	CLOSURE

Magnotta is Ontario's third-largest winery, and, according to the company website, is the only company in Canada licensed to both produce and sell wine, beer and distilled products. While that may sound like a company too big to care about whether it makes good-quality stuff, this line of G. Marquis wines—a spin-off of Magnotta's core winemaking business—proves otherwise. This rich, smoky, well-balanced Pinot Noir features notes of cherries, cinnamon and vanilla.

TRIVIA A marquis is a European nobleman. He ranks above count, but below a duke.

PAIR WITH Roast lamb, grilled salmon, meaty pasta dishes, mushroom risotto.

UNCORK With European nobility, of course, or maybe just your own aristocratic clan. Good for Christmas, Thanksgiving, Canada Day, any day.

MISSION HILL

Mission Hill Family Estate	Reserve	
WINERY	WINE NAME	
Shiraz	2009	
VARIETY	YEAR	
Okanagan Valley, BC, Canada	$25	
ORIGIN	PRICE	CLOSURE

Year after year, from its lofty perch overtop the valley, Mission Hill manages to be one of the most consistent players in the Okanagan, no matter what the weather has been like. This Shiraz is powerful and stylish, with savoury notes of white pepper, dark berries and mocha. Such a treat—it looks and tastes more expensive than it actually is.

The winery is already an impressive tour stop if you're in the Okanagan, but expansion plans are underway for a world-class health spa, high-end hotel and business centre.

TRIVIA Anthony von Mandl, the owner of Mission Hill, also created Mike's Hard Lemonade.

PAIR WITH Roast turkey, lamb or beef dishes. Or just enjoy by itself. Drink now or cellar for a few years.

UNCORK Dinner with the boss, Grandma's birthday, Christmas Day, Thanksgiving, any time you need an impressive red.

TRIOMPHE

Southbrook Vineyards	Triomphe	
WINERY	WINE NAME	
Cabernet Sauvignon/Merlot	2007	
VARIETY	YEAR	
Niagara-on-the-Lake, Canada	$23	
ORIGIN	PRICE	CLOSURE

Southbrook Vineyards is an ultra-modern, all-organic and biodynamic winery started in Ontario by Marilyn and Bill Redelmeier more than 20 years ago. (Bill is apparently "the chief storyteller.") The winemaking team is led by Ann Sperling, one of the legends of Canadian winemaking. Sperling—who was born in Kelowna, BC—made wine at CedarCreek in BC when that winery was just getting off the ground.

Anything but a wallflower, this Cab-Merlot blend (the last non-organic vintage) is leathery and spicy, with a hint of mocha, too.

TRIVIA The name Triomphe comes from the Latin word *triomphus*, which was a song that praised Bacchus, the ancient Greek god of wine.

PAIR WITH Grilled meats, roast lamb. Or just enjoy by itself.

UNCORK With "good company," according to the label! Also, according to the Southbrook website, "the perfect match for enchanted evenings of candlelight and romance." Or Grandma's birthday. Or Christmas Eve. Or cellar for a few years.

CANEPA NOVÍSIMO

Canepa	Novísimo	
WINERY	WINE NAME	
Carménère	2010	
VARIETY	YEAR	
Rapel Valley, Chile	$12	
ORIGIN	PRICE	CLOSURE

Canepa was started in 1930 by one José Canepa Vacarezza, who moved to Chile from Italy, but brought along his love for great vino. Carménère has its roots in France's Bordeaux wine region, but in the past few years Chile has claimed it as its own favourite grape. And when you can make examples of it that taste this good, why not? Expect a big, bold, spicy, earthy red with great tannins and plenty of dark fruit notes.

TRIVIA Winemaking in Chile dates back to the 1500s, when Spanish *conquistadores* brought *Vitis vinifera* (aka wine) grapes with them during their forays around what is now South America.

PAIR WITH Steak, lamb, game, burgers, bison.

UNCORK Large gatherings, tailgate parties.

CASILLERO DEL DIABLO

Concha y Toro	Casillero del Diablo	
WINERY	WINE NAME	
Merlot	2011	
VARIETY	YEAR	
Rapel Valley, Chile	$16	
ORIGIN	PRICE	CLOSURE

Especially renowned for its reds, Concha y Toro is one of Chile's top wineries. The winemaking team produces some incredible high-end wines (don't miss an opportunity to try the Don Melchor, should someone one day offer you a bottle), but it also produces excellent juice for considerably less cash. Take this saucy crowd-pleaser, for instance. *Diablo* means "devil" in Spanish, but don't be scared. This devilishly good red is juicy and delicious, and it's a great bargain for casual Fridays with friends or mid-week indulgences. Expect plummy, fruity, spicy flavours with just a hint of cocoa and soft tannins.

TRIVIA This winery's name, Concha y Toro, means "the seashell and the bull."

PAIR WITH Hard cheese, pasta, roast leg of lamb, pizza, burgers, barbecue, roast chicken, roast Mediterranean-style vegetables or—according to the folks at the winery—Mexican cuisine. Or just enjoy it by itself.

UNCORK Halloween, hockey playoffs, tailgate parties, mid-week gatherings.

MAX RESERVA

Viña Errázuriz	Max Reserva	
WINERY	WINE NAME	
Cabernet Sauvignon	2010	
VARIETY	YEAR	
Valle de Aconcagua, Chile	$21	
ORIGIN	PRICE	CLOSURE

Five generations of the Errázuriz family have headed up this winery, one of Chile's best-known estates. These days, the chief family member is Eduardo Chadwick, an engineer by trade who, among his many accomplishments, partnered on a wine label with Robert Mondavi a few years ago.

This gorgeous Cabernet Sauvignon—from the Max Reserva line—tastes much more expensive than it really is. This full-bodied, handsome red features layer after layer of complex flavours—vanilla, cocoa, cinnamon, red and black fruits and fine tannins, with just enough acidity.

Decant for a bit before serving, so the wine tastes its best, or cellar for a few years, maybe more.

TRIVIA Don Maximiano Errázuriz, the winery's founder and this wine's namesake, was a famous (and wealthy) Chilean politician who owned a copper mining company. At one point, he backed up his government by lending it money. His own money.

PAIR WITH Beef Wellington, steak, goose, game, red meats with red wine sauce, port sauce or mushroom sauce.

UNCORK Fancy dinner parties, dinner with the boss, impressing wine geeks.

BILA-HAUT

M. Chapoutier	Les Vignes de Bila-Haut	
WINERY	WINE NAME	
Carignan/Syrah/Grenache	2009	$20
VARIETY	YEAR	PRICE
Côtes du Roussillon Villages, France		
ORIGIN		CLOSURE

The Chapoutier family motto is "do and hope"—appropriate, really, for a family of winemakers. They're obviously doing something right—they've had vineyards in France since 1808, and M. Chapoutier is easily one of France's best-known wineries. Michel Chapoutier is the man at the helm of the winery, which has vineyards across the country. This earthy, smooth red blend—from Roussillon—is made of Carignan, Syrah and Grenache.

TRIVIA Every M. Chapoutier wine features Braille on its label as a result of Michel Chapoutier hearing a blind musician friend say how it was to choose wine when you are visually impaired. The company now financially supports projects around the world for people who are visually impaired.

PAIR WITH Red meats, Mediterranean-style vegetable dishes such as ratatouille.

UNCORK Now, with Francophiles, turkey days, family gatherings.

CHATEAU ARGADENS

Chateau Argadens	Bordeaux Superieur	
WINERY	WINE NAME	
Red blend (see below)	2009	
VARIETY	YEAR	
Bordeaux, France	$24	
ORIGIN	PRICE	CLOSURE

This wine appeared in the 2010 edition of *Uncorked!* A blend of Merlot and Cabernet Sauvignon (the top two red wine grapes of Bordeaux) and a little bit of Cabernet Franc, this elegant red is an excellent introduction to Bordeaux wines, considered by hardcore wine experts to be some of the world's greatest vin. The Sichel family, who owns Argadens, also owns Château Palmer and Château Margaux, two of the most famous (and priciest) estates in Bordeaux. Winemaker Benjamin Sichel worked in Napa before returning to the family business.

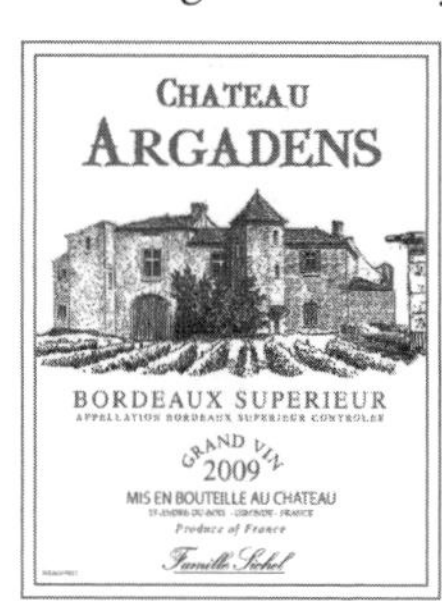

TRIVIA Brits call red Bordeaux "claret," which, if you're pronouncing it correctly, sounds kind of like "carrot."

PAIR WITH Roast beef, steak, lamb.

UNCORK Dinner with wine snobs, dinner with Francophiles. Or cellar for a couple of years.

CHÂTEAU OLLIEUX ROMANIS

Château Ollieux Romanis	Cuvée Classique	
WINERY	WINE NAME	
Carignan/Grenache/Syrah	2009	
VARIETY	YEAR	
Corbières, France	$19	
ORIGIN	PRICE	CLOSURE

Not a lot grows in Corbières, except for grapes, of which most are red. Perfect for wine, too. Take this wine, for instance; it's a blend of mostly Carignan with some Grenache and Syrah. The result is a full-bodied, meaty, savoury, complex red. You get the idea. A whole lot of adjectives that basically mean the wine's worth seeking out.

The winery is owned and operated by a couple who took over the place in the late 1970s, plus their two grown children. Everyone has a role—one's in charge of marketing, another winemaking, another the legal side of the business and still another is in charge of design. They still have a few bottles of wine found buried in sand on the estate that date back to the 19th century.

TRIVIA Peer closely at the label and you'll see the winery's emblem, an olive tree coming out of a crown. The word *ollieux* refers to the handful of olive trees on the estate, some of which have been there for more than 60 years.

PAIR WITH Roast duck, roast chicken or turkey, lamb with herbs.

UNCORK Now, dinner with Francophiles, turkey days, or cellar for a couple of years.

CHATEAU PEY LA TOUR

Chateau Pey La Tour	White Label Series	
WINERY	WINE NAME	
Merlot/Cabernet Sauvignon	2008	
VARIETY	YEAR	
Bordeaux, France	$21	
ORIGIN	PRICE	CLOSURE

Bordeaux is not exactly known as a bargain-hunter's paradise; its red wines are some of the most expensive in the world. This one, however, is a value-priced blend of Merlot and Cabernet Sauvignon. Think of it as learning about Bordeaux on a budget. While there is a yellow label and a white label, the white label is considerably smoother. Both are from a stunningly beautiful estate owned by La Maison Dourthe, a large Bordeaux-based wine company with properties scattered throughout France and, indeed, the world. Back to the wine at hand—Bordeaux blends such as this one do best paired with food, big, meaty dishes or hard cheese.

TRIVIA La Maison Dourthe is also one of the investors in Clos de los Siete, a major wine project in Argentina.

PAIR WITH Red meats, game. Decant this wine for half an hour before serving, or at least leave it open for a while before drinking.

UNCORK With Francophiles, on camping trips, when you're trying to learn more about French wines but don't have enough money to splurge on the major players.

CLOS LA COUTALE

Philippe Bernède	Clos la Coutale	
WINERY	WINE NAME	
Malbec/Merlot	2009	
VARIETY	YEAR	
Cahors, France	$19	
ORIGIN	PRICE	CLOSURE

These days, many of us newbie wine lovers associate the Malbec grape with Argentina. But long before Argentina was famous for its vino, France had its own love affair going on with this inky-hued grape—and much of that affair centred around Cahors, in southwest France. This wine, from a sixth-generation Old World winemaker, is dark, dry, tannic and mysterious, but not inaccessible. Fans of New World wines will appreciate the fact that the blend—mostly of Malbec with a bit of Merlot—still has some flirty, fruity, spicy charm.

TRIVIA In the 1300s, a famous bridge was built in the town. As the legend goes, the builder made a pact with the devil in exchange for help building the bridge. The bridge still stands, but the builder has long since vanished. No word on the devil.

PAIR WITH Cassoulet, frites cooked in duck fat, steak and potatoes.

UNCORK During devilishly good dinner parties with Old World wine fans, storytellers and history buffs.

DOMAINE DE LA CHIQUE

Domaine de la Chique
WINERY

Grenache/Carignan/Syrah	2009	
VARIETY	YEAR	
Côtes du Roussillon, France	$20	
ORIGIN	PRICE	CLOSURE

For a time, this winery—about a 20-minute drive from the city of Perpignan—was the largest olive grove in France. A fellow named Hervé Bizuel—who worked as a sommelier and writer before becoming a winemaker—recognized its significance and saved it from being torn up in 2007. Now his grapes grow between the olives, like a scene from a quirky, beautiful French movie, the kind that makes you want to kiss people on both cheeks. The wine is, as the name suggests, "chic"—sexy and stylish. Made from Grenache (50 percent), with Carignan (30 percent) and old-vine Syrah (20 percent), it has herbal, cherry, mocha and slightly salty notes.

TRIVIA Roussillon fans brag the area is France's warmest, sunniest place, with more than 300 bright days each year.

PAIR WITH Grilled lamb, pork or goat, sausages, salami, roast chicken, anything with olive oil, onions, garlic, roasted tomatoes and herbs. And don't forget to invite me.

UNCORK With wine geeks, Francophiles, chic people—the ones that drink good red and subsist on more than lettuce.

GEORGES DUBŒUF

Georges DuBœuf	Beaujolais-Villages	
WINERY	WINE NAME	
Gamay	2011	
VARIETY	YEAR	
Beaujolais-Villages, France	$16	
ORIGIN	PRICE	CLOSURE

Red wines for white-wine lovers, Beaujolais wines are made from Gamay grapes and are light reds that are rather captivating in their simplicity and their deliciousness. Expect very light tannins and lots of mild strawberry and raspberry notes from this friendly red.

While you'll find both Beaujolais and Beaujolais-Villages wines in Alberta wine shops, the term "Villages" refers to a handful of winemaking towns that produce exceptional (some say superior) Beaujolais.

TRIVIA The third Thursday of every November is Beaujolais Nouveau day, a special day, marked internationally by the release of the latest vintage of Beaujolais. It's a marketing gimmick, true, but it's fun.

PAIR WITH Tuna steaks, salmon, picnic sandwiches.

UNCORK Now, at picnics, casual Fridays, Sunday afternoon lunches.

LOUIS BERNARD

Maison Louis Bernard	Côtes du Rhône Villages	
WINERY	WINE NAME	
Grenache/Syrah	2009	
VARIETY	YEAR	
Rhône Valley, France	$15	
ORIGIN	PRICE	CLOSURE

Make sure this wine says "Côtes du Rhône Villages," because Louis Bernard also has a plain-Jane Côtes du Rhône in our market, and the two bottles look quite similar. You may be tempted because the other one is less expensive, but this one—made from Grenache and Syrah grapes—packs a lot more attitude. (Really. I tasted them both a couple of times while writing this book.) Watch for those herbal and jam notes. This old-school red has lots of tannin, and it will appeal to anyone who loves the romance of Old World wines.

TRIVIA There are 1,837 wineries and 103 wine co-ops throughout the Rhône Valley.

PAIR WITH Prime rib, pork chops, lamb with rosemary.

UNCORK Now, with Francophiles and Old World wine fans. Or stick this one in the cellar for up to three years. It should do just fine.

MALIGNO

Château de Calvières	Maligno	
WINERY	WINE NAME	
Grenache/Syrah/Carignan	2009	
VARIETY	YEAR	
Languedoc-Roussillon, France	$21	
ORIGIN	PRICE	CLOSURE

The French couple behind this wine is living a wine-soaked dream. They gave up demanding careers jet-setting around the world and soon found themselves in a sleepy corner of southwest France. They loved it so much they decided to stay—and, shortly after that, started a winery. Lucky for us. This full-bodied, rich red—a blend of old-vine Grenache, Syrah and Carignan—features spicy chocolate-vanilla-mocha notes. What you need to know? If you like red blends from California, you'll probably like this one.

TRIVIA The winery is in a 12th-century mansion, where Christian knights apparently used to stock up on supplies before heading off to war during the Crusades.

PAIR WITH Smoky barbecued meats, venison, bison burgers.

UNCORK Halloween (of course), with Francophiles and devilishly wonderful friends.

LE MAS

Domaine de Nizas	Le Mas	
WINERY	WINE NAME	
Red blend (see below)	2009	
VARIETY	YEAR	
Languedoc-Roussillon, France	$19	
ORIGIN	PRICE	CLOSURE

The rather youthful Domaine de Nizas winery was started in France in 1998, by the Goelets, a family that also owns the famous Clos du Val winery in Napa Valley, California. The name Le Mas translates from French to English as "the farmhouse" or "little farm." This elegant, full-bodied red is a blend of Cabernet Sauvignon, Syrah and a wee bit of Petit Verdot. Expect red berry fruits and plenty of vanilla and spice notes.

TRIVIA The label features two sculptures by French artist Étienne Maurice Falconet, who made art for Catherine the Great and died in 1791.

PAIR WITH Steaks, French-style stews, roast chicken, roast beef.

UNCORK With wine geeks, Francophiles, California wine buffs and fans of European art.

NOSTRE PAIS

Michel Gassier	Nostre Pais	
WINERY	WINE NAME	
Organic red blend (see below)	2010	
VARIETY	YEAR	
Costières de Nîmes, France	$23	
ORIGIN	PRICE	CLOSURE

Nostre Pais is a small new winery from fourth-generation French winemaker Michel Gassier, whose other projects have included Château de Nâges and Domaine de Molines. If you're only a casual wine lover, you may never have heard of him. But if you're a hardcore wine fan, especially a French wine fan, he'll likely be on your radar.

As for this wine, it's medium-bodied, with notes of rosemary, pencil lead and licorice. A blend of old-vine Carignan, Grenache Noir, Mourvèdre, Cinsault and Syrah, it's velvety smooth, with very mild tannins. Très chic.

Incidentally, Gassier also makes a fine white and rosé under the Nostre Pais label. Beautiful labels, too.

TRIVIA Costières de Nîmes is part of the Rhône Valley and includes the city of Nîmes. The city's coat of arms includes a crocodile chained to a palm tree with the inscription COLNEM, which stands for Colonia Nemausus. The Latin term refers to Nemausus, an ancient Celtic god once revered in the area. Costières de Nîmes also has the best-preserved Roman amphitheatre in France; it's still sometimes used for concerts.

PAIR WITH Simple roast chicken, veal, ratatouille, duck, mildly seasoned lamb roast. Or cellar up to five years.

UNCORK With wine geeks, French wine fans or history buffs, casual Friday gatherings with friends.

PARALLÈLE 45

Paul Jaboulet Aîné	Parallèle 45	
WINERY	WINE NAME	
Grenache/Syrah	2009	
VARIETY	YEAR	
Côtes du Rhône, France	$20	
ORIGIN	PRICE	CLOSURE

One of the best-known names in the Rhône Valley, Paul Jaboulet Aîné is the estate behind this red blend (60 percent Grenache, 40 percent Syrah), which gets its name from the 45th parallel, a circle of latitude that runs just 2 kilometres from the winery's cellars.

While the Paul Jaboulet Aîné estate was started in the early 1800s, a family of champagne producers bought it in 2006; their daughter, Caroline Frey, is now the winemaker for the Paul Jaboulet Aîné wines, too.

As for the wine, it's a bright, cheerful, young red—and a wonderful introduction to what the Rhône has to offer. Its earthy, cherry, spicy notes and its lighter style make it a winner at any latitude.

TRIVIA The 45th parallel also runs through other significant wine regions, including Oregon, Piedmont and southern Ontario. During the summer solstice, at this latitude, the sun is visible for 15 hours and 37 minutes; during the winter solstice, it's visible for 8 hours and 46 minutes.

PAIR WITH Roasted meats, grilled salmon, hard cheeses, stews, tagines.

UNCORK With Francophiles, Sunday dinners, solstice celebrations.

LA VIEILLE FERME

La Vieille Ferme
WINERY

Red blend (see below)	2011	
VARIETY	YEAR	
Côtes du Ventoux, France	$13	
ORIGIN	PRICE	CLOSURE

This wine appeared in the 2010 edition of *Uncorked!* I see a chicken on a wine label, and I immediately start to think about a nice roast chicken and a glass of wine on a Sunday night. Mmm . . . chicken. For those of us who didn't take basic French in high school, *La Vieille Ferme* means "the old farm." But all you really need to know is *bon vin*—good wine. Here's a laid-back wine for those nights when you just feel like hanging out at home and having a glass of red. A blend of Carignan, Cinsault, Grenache and Syrah grapes, this simple, easygoing red has spicy, peppery, fruity notes.

TRIVIA This label was created in 1970 by Jean-Pierre Perrin, whose family also owns Château de Beaucastel, one of Châteauneuf-du-Pape's most legendary estates.

PAIR WITH Grilled chicken (of course!), lasagna, pizza.

UNCORK Going home to the farm, family gatherings, casual Friday nights, casual Sunday dinners.

G.

Ktima Lantides Estate	G.	
WINERY	WINE NAME	
Agiorgitiko	2008	
VARIETY	YEAR	
Nemea, Greece	$18	
ORIGIN	PRICE	CLOSURE

Take a good look at this label. Guess, just guess, how some women like to order it.

That's all I'm saying on that subject. Sure, the gold letter and big spot are attention-getters, but the wine inside is what will make you come back for more. It's big, bold, full of elegance and style, with notes of cherry, cranberry and vanilla. It, um, hits the spot.

Winemaker Panos Lantides studied in Bordeaux before starting his own winery in Greece in 2000. It's a bit of a family affair these days; his son, Andreas, handles North American marketing. As for Panos, he makes wines from a variety of international grapes (Merlot, Cabernet Sauvignon, etc.), as well as Agiorgitiko (St. George), an indigenous Greek variety that's used here. Greek isn't the world's easiest language, and I'm no expert, but try pronouncing Agiorgitiko by saying the letter "g" as a "y."

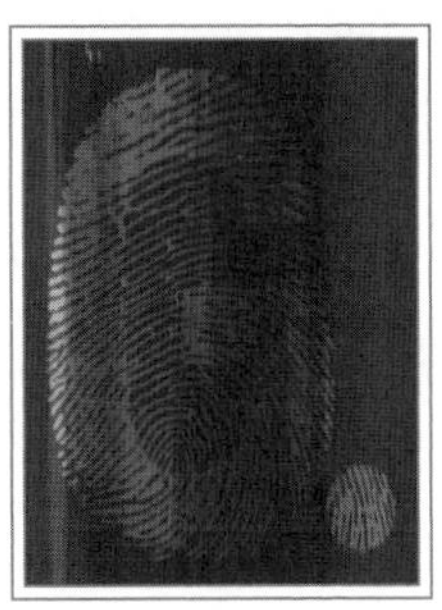

TRIVIA One of the world's most beloved saints, St. George was a Roman soldier who was martyred in AD 303. The grape—Agiorgitiko—named after him is one of Greece's most important indigenous grapes.

PAIR WITH Grilled lamb, prime rib, roasted Mediterranean-style vegetables. Or cellar it for up to six years or so.

UNCORK Christmas Eve, Easter, third dates, any time you feel like doing your bit to relieve the Greek debt crisis.

BRICCOTONDO

Fontanafredda	Briccotondo	
WINERY	WINE NAME	
Barbera	2009	
VARIETY	YEAR	
Piedmont, Italy	$23	
ORIGIN	PRICE	CLOSURE

One of the best-known Italian wineries, Fontanafredda made its mark with its Barolo—earthy, incredible red wines that, well, cost far too much to be included in this book. This savoury, modern sipper is far more affordable and will appeal to everyone—Old World wine fans as well as those of us who grew up downing cheap Shiraz. Barbera is both the type of grape and the style of wine here; while the wine isn't labelled organic, no chemical fertilizers or herbicides were used on the grapes, all grown on the estate.

TRIVIA The first king of Italy, Vittorio Emanuele II, owned the Fontanafredda estate in the 1800s. When he died, his son, who inherited it, created the winery's first Barolo—one of the world's most famous wines.

PAIR WITH Gnocchi, lasagna, mushroom risotto.

UNCORK Friday nights with friends, any time you wish you could go to Italy but can't.

CERASUOLO DI VITTORIA

Feudo di Santa Tresa	Cerasuolo di Vittoria	
WINERY	WINE NAME	
Nero d'Avola/Frappato	2008	
VARIETY	YEAR	
Vittoria, Sicily, Italy	$23	
ORIGIN	PRICE	CLOSURE

This wine appeared in the 2010 edition of *Uncorked!* Mount Etna, an active volcano, dominates the island of Sicily, south of mainland Italy. Perhaps because of Etna's rich, rocky soils, the volcano's slopes have become home to some pretty incredible wineries. Many aficionados consider the Cerasuolo di Vittoria from Feudo di Santa Tresa to be one of Sicily's best; like other Cerasuolos, it's made from Nero d'Avola and Frappato grapes. Look for notes of earth, mint, eucalyptus and berry.

TRIVIA Saint Teresa was a Carmelite nun who lived in the 1500s. She practised discalceation—a fancy word that means she went barefoot for spiritual reasons. She obviously never visited Alberta in January, when people wear shoes for practical reasons.

PAIR WITH Roast lamb, roast chicken, grilled tuna, grilled eggplant, red pepper dishes.

UNCORK All Saints Day, Sunday dinner, with wine geeks.

GABBIANO

Castello di Gabbiano	Chianti Classico	
WINERY	WINE NAME	
Sangiovese	2009	
VARIETY	YEAR	
Tuscany, Italy	$20	
ORIGIN	PRICE	CLOSURE

The pretty-as-a-picture Gabbiano estate is about a half-hour's drive from Florence, in a part of Tuscany known by wine lovers as Chianti Classico. Sangiovese is the official grape of the region and, according to Italian law, at least 80 percent of a Chianti Classico wine must be made from the dark-skinned grape. As you may have guessed, then, this wine is made from Sangiovese. Ready to drink now, it's young and fresh, and while it can be enjoyed by itself, it is served best with food. Those Italians—they know how to make a meal special.

TRIVIA The knight on the Gabbiano label is a reproduction of an image found on the remains of an ancient fresco at the estate.

PAIR WITH Tomato-based pastas, pizza, steak, game dishes.

UNCORK Any time you're serving Italian cuisine, any time you wish you could run away to Tuscany and live *la dolce vita* every day.

IL LABIRINTO

Fattoria Poggerino	Il Labirinto	
WINERY	WINE NAME	
Organic Sangiovese	2010	
VARIETY	YEAR	
Tuscany, Italy	$22	
ORIGIN	PRICE	CLOSURE

This wine appeared in the 2010 edition of *Uncorked!* Winemaker Pierro Lanza and his sister Benedetta are behind this small but highly regarded organic winery in the heart of the Chianti Classico wine region, near Radda in Chianti. They operate a small bed and breakfast, too; go to poggerino.com for information. But back to the wine—indeed, every wine Lanza turns his mind to making is worth checking out, probably because he is as devoted to his vineyards as he is to the winery. This multi-layered Sangiovese is mighty fine now, but it'll handle some time in the cellar, too.

TRIVIA The word Sangiovese comes from the Latin term *sanguis Jovis*, which literally means "the blood of Jove." In Roman mythology, Jove, aka Jupiter, is the king of the gods and the god of thunder. And labyrinths have long been spiritually significant; walk into the heart of a labyrinth to find your inner self. Ponder that while you sip and stare at the label.

PAIR WITH Parmigiano Reggiano, Tuscan-style bread with salt and olive oil, charcuterie (a platter of ham, salami and other cold cuts), risotto, grilled lamb.

UNCORK Now, with wine geeks, Italophiles or spiritually minded wine lovers.

MASI CAMPOFIORIN

Masi	Campofiorin	
WINERY	WINE NAME	
Corvina/Rondinella/Molinara	2008	
VARIETY	YEAR	
Veneto, Italy	$22	
ORIGIN	PRICE	CLOSURE

This wine appeared in the 2010 edition of *Uncorked!* Some of the first red wines that I drank and liked came from Masi. Approximately 100 years later, I still feel that way—I know that I'm getting a reliable, well-made wine at a good price. This rich, complex, dark red—sometimes referred to as a super Venetian—is loaded with plummy, jammy, smoky, sweetish flavours and smooth tannins. It's made in the Ripasso style, which means it's made from vino that has been "repassed" over a percentage of lightly dried grapes, similar to the way that Amarone (a rich, expensive Italian red wine) is made. Although many Veneto wineries now make the style, Masi claims to have been the first, in 1964.

TRIVIA Campofiorin literally means "field of flowers."

PAIR WITH Roast beast, hard cheese, hearty risottos. It'll also cellar for a few years.

UNCORK January blizzards, February blizzards, dinner at the boss's house.

PAIARA

Tormaresca	Paiara	
WINERY	WINE NAME	
Negroamaro/Cabernet Sauvignon	2010	
VARIETY	YEAR	
Puglia, Italy	$13	
ORIGIN	PRICE	CLOSURE

Tormaresca is a side project of the legendary Antinori family, who helped to create the super-Tuscan craze with their Tignanello wine, which they first created in the 1970s.

This winery, however, isn't in Tuscany. It's located in Puglia, the southeastern "high heel" of Italy's boot. Paiara refers to straw—in particular, rustic little straw-thatched stone houses found in the region.

This warm, friendly, easy-drinking dark red wine is made from Negroamaro grapes, which are native to southern Italy, plus some Cabernet Sauvignon. Expect lovely soft tannins and plenty of juicy cherry fruit. Yum. A fantastic deal.

TRIVIA About 80 percent of Europe's pasta comes from the Puglia region of Italy; about 80 percent of the country's olive oil also comes from here.

PAIR WITH Grilled chicken, pasta, pizza, burgers.

UNCORK Now, Italian national holidays, book club, mid-week pick-me-ups, large family gatherings.

PLANETA LA SEGRETA

Planeta	La Segreta	
WINERY	WINE NAME	
Red blend (see below)	2010	
VARIETY	YEAR	
Sicily, Italy	$18	
ORIGIN	PRICE	CLOSURE

Perhaps Sicily's most famous and most exciting winery, Planeta was started by three siblings—all still actively involved—in the 1980s. Their success has been phenomenal, and they now own vineyards across the island. While Planeta is best known for some of its pricier wines, wine lovers in search of a deal won't want to miss this entry-level (aka more affordable) red. It's a blend of mostly Nero d'Avola, with some Merlot, Cabernet Franc and Syrah mixed in for good measure.

TRIVIA La Segreta is named after a forested area that surrounds the vineyards where the grapes for this wine are grown.

PAIR WITH Pasta, sausages with fennel, eggplant parmigiana, ratatouille, chicken, salmon.

UNCORK Now, with Italophiles and wine geeks, at family dinners.

PRIMITIVO DEI FEUDI DI SAN GREGORIO

Feudi di San Gregorio
WINERY

Primitivo di Manduria — 2009
VARIETY (AND APPELATION) — YEAR

Puglia, Italy — $20
ORIGIN — PRICE — CLOSURE

This wine appeared in the 2010 edition of *Uncorked!* The Feudi di San Gregorio estate is located on some of the oldest wine-producing land in what is now Italy. Records show that wine grapes were grown there as far back as AD 590—a date considered to be the start of the Middle Ages.

Feudi di San Gregorio was started in the mid-1980s in Campania, which wasn't particularly known for its wines outside of Italy. But the folks at Feudi di San Gregorio—who specialize in showcasing the region's indigenous grapes—have done a lot to put it on the map for wine lovers. Manduria, by the way, is a city located just inside the high heel part of the "boot" that forms the map of Italy.

This wine—made from 100 percent Primitivo—is a big, powerful red with loads of bossy attitude and warm, plummy notes.

TRIVIA Primitivo is the 12th-most-common grape in Italy. Or so they say. It's also Italian for "Zinfandel."

PAIR WITH Italian sausages, meatball sandwiches, steak, short ribs.

UNCORK For NHL playoffs, dinners with Italophiles, dinner with wine geeks.

R

Alpha Zeta	R	
WINERY	WINE NAME	
Corvina/Rondinella	2010	
VARIETY	YEAR	
Valpolicella, Veneto, Italy	$22	
ORIGIN	PRICE	CLOSURE

This wine appeared in the 2010 edition of *Uncorked!* Sometimes referred to as a "baby Amarone," a Ripasso wine is made when a winemaker takes a young red wine and blends it ("repasses" it over) the leftover dried grapes and skins from the Amarone winemaking process, which involves making a very concentrated, rich red wine from partially dried grapes. A Ripasso wine offers a lot of the same rich taste of an Amarone, but at a fraction of the price—just what we bargain wine hunters want to know. Alpha Zeta may be located in Italy, but the winemaker, Matt Thomson, is actually from New Zealand. He splits his time between the two countries, making wine in both places.

TRIVIA This winery was started by David Gleave, who was born and raised in Toronto. Gleave is a Master of Wine (less than 10 Canadians share this distinction) and lives in London, England, where he's a founder and managing director for Liberty Wines.

PAIR WITH Braised meats, Italian feasts. Or just enjoy it by itself.

UNCORK Snowy nights, big family gatherings, winter solstice celebrations, with friends who still think a big jammy Australian Shiraz is the be-all and end-all of good wine. Show 'em there's more to life.

RÈMOLE

Frescobaldi	Rèmole	
WINERY	WINE NAME	
Sangiovese/Cabernet Sauvignon	2009	
VARIETY	YEAR	
Tuscany, Italy	$12	
ORIGIN	PRICE	CLOSURE

The Frescobaldi family—Italian nobility—has been making wine in Italy's Tuscany region for more than 700 years. (That's 30 generations. Yes, 30.) This wine—a blend of Sangiovese and Cabernet Sauvignon—is named after Villa Rèmole, a house on one of the family's properties where descendants of those long-ago Frescobaldis still live. This ultra-smooth, easy-drinking red is a real crowd-pleaser and is very food friendly. One to buy by the armload if you're holding a big party on a budget.

TRIVIA The Frescobaldis supplied wine to King Henry VIII and Michelangelo, who traded his paintings for wine. No word on how many bottles per masterpiece.

PAIR WITH Hard cheese, steak, risotto, pasta, meatloaf, pizza.

UNCORK Family gatherings, Friday night dinners. Or cellar for a couple of years.

SASYR

Rocca delle Macie	Sasyr	
WINERY	WINE NAME	
Sangiovese/Syrah	2008	
VARIETY	YEAR	
Tuscany, Italy	$20	
ORIGIN	PRICE	CLOSURE

This wine appeared in the 2010 edition of *Uncorked!* "Super Tuscan" doesn't just refer to a really nice person from central Italy. It's also a trendy name given to wines—often very expensive wines—from (big surprise here) Tuscany. They don't follow traditional Chianti Classico (aka Tuscan) blending laws, though, because they're throwing in grapes that aren't common to the region—Merlot, for instance, or, in this case, Syrah.

As for the name Sasyr, it comes from the wine's grapes—"Sa" for Sangiovese and "Syr" for Syrah, which is just another name for Shiraz.

TRIVIA Ever watched a spaghetti western? Italo Zingarelli, the guy who started Rocca delle Macie, was one of their producers. One of his most famous was They Call Me Trinity. His son and granddaughter are now heavily involved in operating the winery, which offers gorgeous on-site lodgings, as well.

PAIR WITH Grilled meat, hard cheese, Italian sausage.

UNCORK During rodeo season, any time you feel like shooting a pistol, wearing a cowboy hat or riding off into the sunset.

ZENATO RIPASSA

Zenato	Ripassa
WINERY	WINE NAME
Corvina/Rondinella/Molinara	2009
VARIETY	YEAR
Valpolicella, Veneto, Italy	$25
ORIGIN	PRICE

CLOSURE

This wine appeared in the 2010 edition of *Uncorked!* Ripassa wines developed out of the process used to make the fabulously rich and pricey Amarone wines—also from this area of Italy. First, the grapes—Corvina, Rondinella and Molinara—are let to dry until they have almost turned into raisins. Then that pulp is passed over (*ripassa*, as the Italians would say) with younger wine. The result is a dark, rich wine with silky tannins and tons of flavour. It's tough to find a ripassa-style wine that costs $25 or less, especially one of this quality, from a family-owned winery. Pardon the pun, but don't pass this one up.

TRIVIA Veneto is Italy's most-visited region. Every year, more than 13.5 million tourists come for the food, the wine and, of course, the romantic beauty of cities like Venice and Verona.

PAIR WITH Italian feasts, braised meats, stewy dishes.

UNCORK First snowfalls, January blizzards, spring snowstorms, dinners with Italophiles. Or stick in the cellar for up to five years.

OPAWA

Nautilus Winery	Opawa	
WINERY	WINE NAME	
Pinot Noir	2009	
VARIETY	YEAR	
Marlborough, New Zealand	$18	
ORIGIN	PRICE	CLOSURE

A secondary project from the folks at New Zealand's Nautilus Winery, the Opawa wines cost slightly less but offer excellent value. Opawa means "smoky river" in Maori; that's also the name of the vineyard where the grapes for this wine are grown. A fellow named Brett Birmingham is the winemaker, and while he may not be a household name to NZ wine lovers, he cut his winemaking teeth at Cloudy Bay—one of the country's most famous wineries. This wine is just what you'd expect from a high-quality New Zealand Pinot Noir—juicy cherry and plum notes, with cinnamon and vanilla notes.

TRIVIA There are about 660,000 Maori living in New Zealand—about 15 percent of the country's population.

PAIR WITH Cedar-planked salmon, grilled chicken, duck.

UNCORK During a full moon or the last quarter, while watching New Zealand rugby games on TV.

12,000 MILES

Gladstone Vineyards	12,000 Miles	
WINERY	WINE NAME	
Organic Pinot Noir	2011	
VARIETY	YEAR	
Gladstone, New Zealand	$23	
ORIGIN	PRICE	CLOSURE

Gladstone's Christine Kernohan is apparently one of only three female Scottish winemakers in the world. The name of the wine—12,000 Miles—represents the distance between Scotland and New Zealand, where Kernohan and her husband moved in the 1970s with their daughters. They're in Gladstone, an up-and-coming wine region on New Zealand's North Island. This lush Pinot Noir—both organic and biodynamic—is savoury and spicy, with dark fruity, cherry notes.

TRIVIA According to a 2009 study by Health Scotland, the average Scottish person buys three bottles of wine per week. But does it go into the cellar?

PAIR WITH Roast leg of lamb with rosemary, pork loin, grilled chicken or duck.

UNCORK After long trips, clan gatherings, Robbie Burns Day (it's more affordable than Scotch).

WHITEHAVEN

Whitehaven
WINERY

Pinot Noir — VARIETY
2009 — YEAR

Marlborough, New Zealand — ORIGIN
$24 — PRICE
CLOSURE

I always love stories like this one—the couple who started this winery fled high-powered careers in finance and marketing to pursue the bucolic winery life in New Zealand. (Translation—they probably worked even harder at the winery, but at least they could drink something delicious that they'd made at the end of their day.) Marlborough—perhaps New Zealand's most famous wine region—is especially renowned for its Sauvignon Blanc wines, but delicious Pinot Noir, such as this one, is certainly worth checking out. Expect tons of spicy cherry notes—true-to-form Pinot Noir, and it's tasty, too.

TRIVIA New Zealand was the first country in the world to give women the right to vote, and it was the first country to introduce retirement pensions—just in case you needed more reasons to love the place after trying its outrageously good wines.

PAIR WITH Grilled salmon, roast chicken, roast turkey.

UNCORK Turkey days, Sunday dinners, casual dinners with friends.

CRASTO

Quinta do Crasto	Crasto
WINERY	WINE NAME
Red blend (see below)	2010
VARIETY	YEAR
Douro Valley, Portugal	$20
ORIGIN	PRICE

CLOSURE

This wine appeared in the 2010 edition of *Uncorked!* Many of the grapes in this wine—Tinta Barroca, Touriga Franca and Touriga Nacional—are indigenous Portuguese grapes. While they may not exactly be household names for wine lovers in Canada, they certainly have an important place in the world of wine. Not only are they made into the country's famous port, but they also make a personality-packed dark red table wine. This one—from a family-owned winery with roots dating back to the 1600s—is savoury and powerful, with good fruity notes and smooth tannins.

TRIVIA All of Quinta do Crasto's wines are made the old-fashioned way; the grapes are first stomped by foot in granite tanks.

PAIR WITH Paella, spicy Spanish chorizo sausage, roasted Mediterranean-style vegetables.

UNCORK Camping trips, Friday night barbecues with friends.

ALENTO

Adega do Monte Branco	Alento	
WINERY	WINE NAME	
Red blend (see below)	2010	
VARIETY	YEAR	
Alentejo, Portugal	$22	
ORIGIN	PRICE	CLOSU

Adega do Monte Branco is a rather young winery located in the south-central part of Portugal. Luis Louro grew up in the wine industry; his family owns an old-school winery in the same region, and he worked there for several years before striking out on his own to create something a bit more modern and fresh. Still, he doesn't ignore his roots; the grapes for this full-bodied red are crushed by foot, and they include a slew of interesting regional grapes, including Touriga Nacional, Aragonez, Alicante Bouschet and Trincadeira. Study those, just in case there's a test later. Expect a spicy, plummy, rather savoury wine with lots of flavour and body.

TRIVIA *Alento* is a Portuguese word that means "inspiration, spirit and courage."

PAIR WITH Paella, rice and beans, steak and other beefy dishes.

UNCORK With good friends and courageous company, inspiring dinners.

CATHEDRAL CELLAR TRIPTYCH

KWV	Cathedral Cellar Triptych	
WINERY	WINE NAME	
Cabernet Sauvignon/Merlot/Shiraz	2008	
VARIETY	YEAR	
Paarl, Western Cape, South Africa	$19	
ORIGIN	PRICE	CLOSURE

The letters KWV stand for "Kooperratiewe Wijnbouwers-vereniging." Got that? There's a spelling test later. Seriously, KWV is a South African cooperative that started in 1918 and now includes a ton of big brands. One of those labels, Cathedral Cellar, was named after the winery's vaulted-roof cellar, which was built in 1930. Wine geeks say this blend is made from "noble" grapes, a term that has little to do with royalty and everything to do with which grapes the experts think are the best—stuff like Cabernet Sauvignon and Merlot. They're the famous grapes, really, the ones that manage to be both the rock stars and the workhorses of the wine world. Here, they make a shiny big red with tons of spice and fruit, plus smooth tannins, the stuff that gives you that dry sensation in your mouth when you drink red wine.

TRIVIA A triptych is a piece of artwork that is divided into three sections.

PAIR WITH Grilled meats, grilled vegetables. Or just enjoy by itself.

UNCORK When your South African friends invite you over for a *braai*, a typical South African outdoor barbecue party.

THE DEN

Painted Wolf Wines	The Den	
WINERY	WINE NAME	
Pinotage	2010	
VARIETY	YEAR	
Coastal Region, South Africa	$15	
ORIGIN	PRICE	CLOSURE

Pinotage isn't always the easiest grape to love, even if you're a red wine drinker. Trust me: I tried a ton in my search for good ones for this book.

But here's an example of it at its best, an easy-drinking, slightly smoky, savoury, medium-bodied red that has an outgoing, uncomplicated personality, and is as charming as a passel of newborn puppies.

And it's a feel-good wine, too. Painted Wolf gets its name from endangered African wild dogs of the same name. Through wine sales, winery staff financially support charities in Africa that aim to protect these indigenous dogs.

TRIVIA A South African scientist created Pinotage in 1925, as a cross between Pinot Noir and Cinsault grapes. Since then it has become South Africa's signature red.

PAIR WITH Smoky sausages, slow-roasted ribs, homemade burgers, steak or other red meat dishes.

UNCORK Dog day afternoons (and evenings), barbecues, dog show after-parties (if there aren't such things, there should be).

GLEN CARLOU

Glen Carlou
WINERY

Syrah
VARIETY

2007
YEAR

Paarl Valley, South Africa
ORIGIN

$20
PRICE

CLOSURE

Paarl—a derivative of the Dutch word for "pearl"—is one of South Africa's major wine regions. (Also in the region is the city of Paarl, South Africa's third-largest city.) The Glen Carlou winery is owned by Hess Family Estates, a Swiss investment team and family who own wineries around the world. As for this Syrah, it features beautiful savoury, peppery, blackcurrant and vanilla notes.

TRIVIA Winemaking in South Africa dates back to the 1600s, when a group of Protestants called Huguenots—fleeing pro-Catholic persecution in France—immigrated to the country, bringing their own food and wine traditions.

PAIR WITH Grilled red meat, roast chicken, mild Italian-style sausage, cassoulet. Or cellar for a year or two.

UNCORK Saturday night dinners with friends, watching World Cup soccer games or rugby matches.

THE GRINDER

The Grape Grinder	The Grinder	
WINERY	WINE NAME	
Pinotage	2011	
VARIETY	YEAR	
Western Cape, South Africa	$18	
ORIGIN	PRICE	CLOSURE

You'll know exactly why this wine has its name (and why it has the old-school hand-cranked grinder on the label) as soon as you take a sip. Its big, bold, mocha notes will immediately make coffee aficionados think of brewing up a fresh pot of joe. Mmm. So rich and intense, you'll almost want to chew it. There's no actual coffee in this wine, however; the flavour comes from the Pinotage grape and the way the wine is made. It spends time in oak, which gives vanilla hints to the wine, and it uses a special type of yeast that, in combination with the Pinotage grape, leads to rich espresso flavours.

TRIVIA Coffee grinders, sometimes called "mills," have been used in North America since the 1700s, but the box-mill grinders, like the kind shown on the label, probably came on the scene in the early 1800s, according to Robert Doerr and Robert Stienke at coffeehouseinc.com.

PAIR WITH Smoky, sticky pork ribs; barbecued meats of all kinds.

UNCORK Rugby matches, hockey playoffs, camping trips, for fans of big jammy Australian Shiraz, days when you realize you've downed an entire pot of coffee—and you wish you had more.

OBIKWA

Obikwa
WINERY

Shiraz — VARIETY
2010 — YEAR

Western Cape, South Africa — ORIGIN
$10 — PRICE
CLOSURE

One of the most affordable wines in the book, Obikwa has been a standby for bargain-wine hunters around the world, since the winery was started in 2002. While the wine isn't organic, it is created with eco-friendly practices in mind. The bottles, for instance, are extra-thin, meaning that they're lighter and use less fuel to ship. That's an especially big deal if you consider that Obikwa wines are sold in more than 43 countries.

Expect medium tannins and a big whollop of sweet, jammy fruit. A tasty crowd-pleaser. Keep it on hand for those mid-week dinners when you want to open a bottle, but you don't want to feel guilty for wasting money if you don't finish the entire thing.

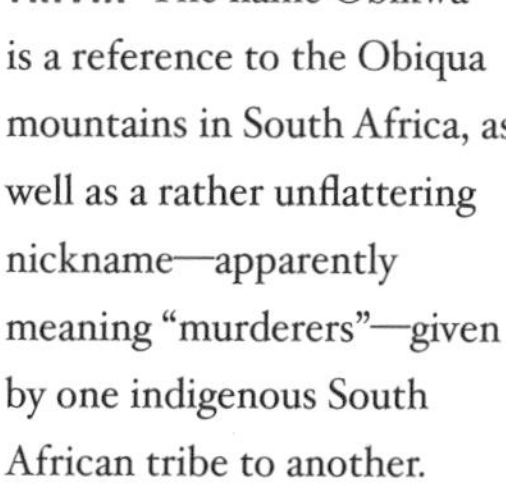

TRIVIA The name Obikwa is a reference to the Obiqua mountains in South Africa, as well as a rather unflattering nickname—apparently meaning "murderers"—given by one indigenous South African tribe to another.

PAIR WITH Pizza, meatloaf, burgers, fajitas, lasagna, roast beast of any kind.

UNCORK Tailgate parties, camping trips, watching UFC fight nights on the big screen, any time you're saving for something major but want a reliable wine and some fun.

THE WOLFTRAP

Boekenhoutskloof	The Wolftrap	
WINERY	WINE NAME	
Syrah/Mourvèdre/Viognier	2011	
VARIETY	YEAR	
Western Cape, South Africa	$14	
ORIGIN	PRICE	CLOSURE

This wine appeared in the 2010 edition of *Uncorked!* Pronounced *Book-en-HOOTS-kloof*, this spicy blockbuster blend—Syrah, Mourvèdre and Viognier—delivers a wallop of vanilla, chocolate, berries and spice. Satisfying and sexy. And just in case you care, wine geeks call this a Rhône-style blend, a reference to the fact that it's made like wines from France's Rhône Valley.

TRIVIA No wolf, real or otherwise, has ever been captured or, for that matter, even seen in the valley at Boekenhoutskloof, where this wine was made. There is, however, a 250-year-old trap. Just in case.

PAIR WITH Barbecue, tagine, ribs, pizza, burgers, bison, venison. Or just enjoy by itself.

UNCORK With Little Red Riding Hood's Grandma, with men named Peter, while listening to Howlin' Wolf, Steppenwolf or Los Lobos (Spanish for "wolves").

BESO DE VINO

Grandes Vinos y Viñedos	Beso de Vino	
WINERY	WINE NAME	
Old Vine Garnacha	2009	
VARIETY	YEAR	
Cariñena, Spain	$14	
ORIGIN	PRICE	CLOSURE

When you try this wine, don't think of bullfights, despite the cartoon bull (whose name is apparently Antonio) on the label. The word *beso* means "kiss" in Spanish, and that's exactly what this wine is—a fun peck on the cheek. Nothing serious, just flirty and fun. Founded in 1997, this winery is a mere infant compared with many Spanish bodegas. The vineyards, however, go back 40 years or more, meaning that this medium-bodied, garnet-hued wine comes from "old vines." They're gnarly, thick and weathered and, because of their age, they produce intensely flavoured berries that make intensely flavoured wine. Known as Grenache in France, the grape is called Garnacha in Spain.

TRIVIA There are three tiny holes in the aluminum cap and, inside that cap, a "controlled permeability membrane" that allows a bit of oxygen to reach the wine, just enough to ensure you'll enjoy some smooth, easy-drinking juice. Instead of recycling the bottle when you're finished, you could always pop out the membrane and create one very big salt shaker.

PAIR WITH Tomatoey pastas, pizza, burgers, cheese, beef.

UNCORK World Cup soccer games, casual Fridays with friends, mid-week dinners, first dates.

LA CASONA DE CASTAÑO

Familia Castaño	La Casona de Castaño	
WINERY	WINE NAME	
Old Vines Monastrell	2009	
VARIETY	YEAR	
Yecla, Spain	$12	
ORIGIN	PRICE	CLOSURE

This family-owned winery has a few different vinos in the Alberta market, and they're all great, but this one stands out because it's extra, extra-good value. Low price. Tons of fine flavours.

The grapes used to make this wine all come from dry-farmed vines, all at least 40 to 60 years old. Dry-farming means the wines aren't irrigated—and the result means intensely flavoured grapes. Same with the old vines. They produce fewer grapes, but what they do make is deliciously intense.

TRIVIA Casona means "big house" in Spanish, and it's a nod to the old farmhouses that surround the vineyards in the region. In ancient times, people would live in those houses, sometimes having to share space with their mules and other animals.

PAIR WITH Meaty dishes, charcuterie (a fancy word for European cold cuts). Or just enjoy by itself.

UNCORK World Cup soccer games, tax season, RRSP season, housewarming parties.

G

Compañía de Vinos Telmo Rodriguez

WINERY

G Dehesa Gago	Tinta de Toro	2010
WINE NAME	VARIETY	YEAR
Toro, Spain	$18	
ORIGIN	PRICE	CLOSURE

This wine appeared in the 2010 edition of *Uncorked!* Telmo Rodriguez is a rock star when it comes to the world's winemakers. Imagine, for a minute, Chris Martin, the lead vocalist from Coldplay. You know he has a slew of awesome musicians playing with him, but, well, it's Chris—charismatic, slightly angsty, mysterious and brilliant—that's the household name.

Telmo Rodriguez is like that. He makes wine in 10 different regions in Spain—hence his title, "the driving winemaker." The Dehesa Gago comes from Toro, a region that isn't as famous as, say, Rioja, but is still cranking out some very tasty stuff. As for the grape here, Tinta de Toro, most experts are hard pressed to tell the difference between it and Tempranillo. Expect a food-friendly, earthy, savoury, complex red, with a finish that just goes on and on.

TRIVIA Rodriguez met his winemaking partner, Pablo Eguzkiza, when the two studied and worked together in Bordeaux, France. Eguzkiza—who was top of his class at wine school—worked at France's Château Pétrus, one of the world's greatest wineries, before coming to make wine with his buddy Rodriguez.

PAIR WITH Beef, lamb dishes, roast pork.

UNCORK Dinners with wine geeks, bullfights (*toro* also means "bull" in Spanish), Ultimate Fighting Championships (the closest thing we have in Canada to bullfights), rodeos, barbecues. Or cellar for a few years.

LATRIA

Celler Malondro	Latria	
WINERY	WINE NAME	
Garnacha/Cariñena	2008	
VARIETY	YEAR	
Montsant, Spain	$22	
ORIGIN	PRICE	CLOSURE

This small, family winery was started in 2000, and the Montsant appellation was created a year later. The Celler Malondro vineyards, the highest in Montsant, are all at least 40 years old—meaning they officially qualify as old vines, and they now produce grapes that make rich, intensely flavoured wines. Take this well-balanced beauty, for instance. It's subtle and elegant, with notes of cherry, lavender, spice and minerals. Something else I love about it? It only spends about six months in old oak, so the taste of the fruit isn't overpowered by too many toasty, oaky, vanilla flavours.

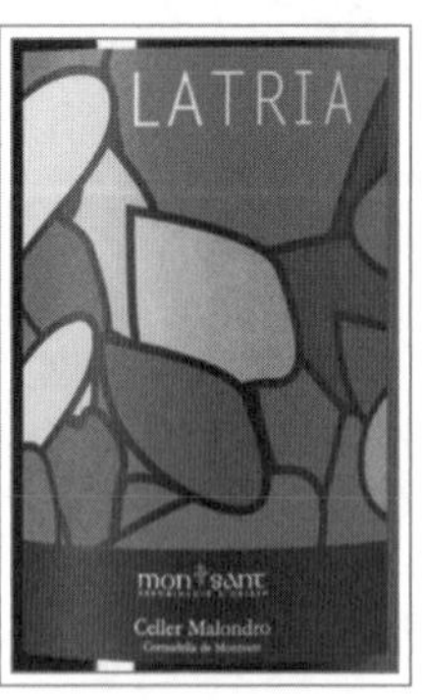

TRIVIA The word *latria* is actually Latin and means "adoration." A great word to describe what I felt when I first tried this wine.

PAIR WITH Roast chicken, game, red meat, roasted Mediterranean-style vegetables, homemade garlic sausage.

UNCORK Chick nights; dinner with wine snobs, Old World wine fans, someone you adore.

LOS 800

Los 800
WINERY

Red blend (see below)	2007	
VARIETY	YEAR	
Priorat, Spain	$23	
ORIGIN	PRICE	CLOSURE

In the past 20 years or so, Priorat has become famous for its big, very expensive red wines. It's rare, if not impossible, to find something from the region that's value-priced. And when you do come across a wine like this, which is the same price as 5 lattes, not 50? You rejoice, that's what. This gem of a bottle is complex and exciting, with savoury, earthy notes of graphite, licorice, herbs and cherry. Oh yeah, there are tons of fine tannins, too, if you care. The grapes? A blend of Garnacha, Cariñena, Cabernet Sauvignon and Syrah.

TRIVIA The name Los 800 comes from the fact that this winery only sources grapes from old vineyards at least 800 metres above sea level. Just in case it comes up at your next dinnertime conversation.

PAIR WITH Lamb, souvlaki, venison, bison burgers, charcuterie.

UNCORK With wine geeks, watching FIFA World Cup soccer games.

LUJURIA

Bodegas Castaño	Lujuria	
WINERY	WINE NAME	
Monastrell/Merlot	2011	
VARIETY	YEAR	
Yecla, Spain	$15	
ORIGIN	PRICE	CLOSURE

This wine appeared in the 2010 edition of *Uncorked!* This label is so pretty and simple (designed by Vancouver's Jennifer Delf, a self-described bird lover and the wine's importer), maybe you'll underestimate the wine within the bottle. But it's delicious. A blend of Monastrell (aka Mourvèdre) and Merlot, this easy-drinking red wine has smoky, fruity notes and nice, soft tannins, so drink it now. I am. It hails from a wine region called Yecla, located in southeastern Spain.

TRIVIA Google "lujuria" and you'll find . . . well, on second thought, you may just want to know that the word *lujuria* means "lust" in Spanish. You might lust after this wine once you try a glass or two.

PAIR WITH Grilled meat (even roast chicken), paella, mild Italian sausage.

UNCORK First dates, third dates, hot summer evenings, hump nights, snowstorms.

EL PETIT BONHOMME

Nathalie Bonhomme	El Petit Bonhomme	
WINERY	WINE NAME	
Monastrell/Syrah/Grenache	2010	
VARIETY	YEAR	
Jumilla, Spain	$15	
ORIGIN	PRICE	CLOSURE

Born in Montreal and now living in Spain, Nathalie Bonhomme started her wine path as a marketer. (Wine geeks will want to know she works with Pingus, made by Danish winemaker Peter Sisseck.) Now, with the help of the folks at Bodega Juan Gil (also a wonderful winery), she's making wine, too. This juicy crowd-pleaser features peppery, dark fruit and meaty notes. You can see that the name of the wine has nothing to do with Quebec's cheery snowman. But, like Quebec's snowman, this wine is approachable, interesting and fun, too. Be sure to check out the back of the label.

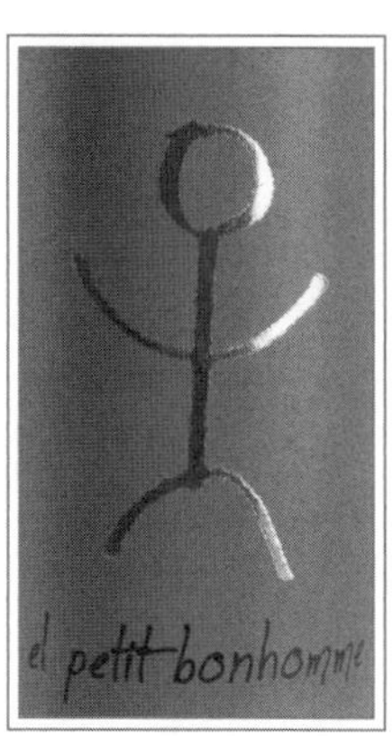

TRIVIA According to the official Quebec Carnaval website, Canada's Bonhomme—the snowman, not the lovely winemaker—is "the living incarnation of the snowmen that have enchanted children of Quebec City for generations." Frankly, I'd rather have wine, not snow.

PAIR WITH Ratatouille, steak, hard cheese, barbecued ribs. Very food friendly and versatile.

UNCORK After snowball fights, during Carnaval.

PLIC PLIC PLIC

Terra de Falanis	Plic Plic Plic	
WINERY	WINE NAME	
Samso/Garnacha	2009	
VARIETY	YEAR	
Montsant, Spain	$16	
ORIGIN	PRICE	CLOSURE

Terra de Falanis is a side project of two intriguing winemakers from Anima Negra, a winery on the Spanish island of Majorca. Their aim is to create value-oriented wines from indigenous grapes. The grapes here aren't exactly indigenous to Spain, but they do make some lovely wine. This playful but chic red blend is made from 50 percent Samso (aka Carignan) and 50 percent Garnacha (aka Grenache). Look for red berry notes with just a hint of mocha. Super smooth and well balanced.

TRIVIA Located on the edge of the mountain region of the same name, Montsant is shaped like a horseshoe, and it encircles Priorat, Spain's priciest wine region.

PAIR WITH Roast meat, charcuterie. Or just enjoy by itself.

UNCORK Fashion shows, dinner with wine geeks, book club gatherings.

LA VENDIMIA

Palacios Remondo	La Vendimia	
WINERY	WINE NAME	
Tempranillo/Garnacha	2010	
VARIETY	YEAR	
Rioja, Spain	$23	
ORIGIN	PRICE	CLOSURE

This wine appeared in the 2010 edition of *Uncorked!* La Vendimia is just as good, if not better, than the first time. The very pretty label—a colourful, stylized tree—may make you wonder if the Rioja inside the bottle is, in fact, as pretty. But it is, a stylish, elegant, fruit-packed spicy wine that's a great one to impress a wine snob, if you don't want to cough up for a pricier bottle. It's made from Tempranillo and Garnacha grapes.

TRIVIA Born into a family that's been making wine for more than 350 years, Alvaro Palacios—one of five boys—spent his childhood playing in his parents' Rioja winery. Now an internationally famous winemaker, he studied in Bordeaux, then made his name with a (considerably more expensive) wine called L'Ermita. As for the word *vendimia*, it's Spanish for "grape harvest" or "vintage."

PAIR WITH Charcuterie (aka cured meats), hard-aged cheddar and Parmesan-style cheeses or red grilled meat.

UNCORK Dinner with the boss, dinner with wine snobs, book club with your best gal pals.

CAMERON HUGHES LOT 313

Cameron Hughes Wines	Lot 313	
WINERY	WINE NAME	
Red blend (see below)	2010	
VARIETY	YEAR	
California, US	$23	
ORIGIN	PRICE	CLOSURE

English major–turned-entrepreneur Cameron Hughes picked up a job selling wine as an easy way to make some cash during university. He quickly realized, however, there was a hole in the market for someone like him, who couldn't afford to buy a winery. He could, however, buy excess wines from other wineries, then rent the space to bottle that wine, repackage it and sell it as his own label. This wine comes from throughout California, the American state where he started his career; it's a big, bold but well-balanced mishmash of Zinfandel, Petite Sirah, Carignan and Syrah.

TRIVIA Cameron Hughes is a negociant, someone who deals in many aspects of wine creation. He buys and sells wine, buys grapes, makes wine, and bottles wine—but he doesn't actually own a winery.

PAIR WITH All kinds of red meat, barbecue, Italian sausage.

UNCORK Dinner with the boss, dinner parties with friends. Or cellar for a couple of years.

CANNONBALL

Cannonball Wine Company
WINERY

Cabernet Sauvignon — VARIETY
2009 — YEAR

Sonoma Coast, California, US — ORIGIN
$25 — PRICE
CLOSURE

This wine appeared in the 2010 edition of *Uncorked!* According to the label, a cannonball "is the perfect symbol of freedom. Legs tucked beneath you, soaring through the air." Well, I don't think you'll turn into the wine lover's equivalent of a Cirque du Soleil performer when you drink this wine, but you will find a big, handsome, full-bodied red wine that's loaded with notes of vanilla, spice and dark fruit.

TRIVIA Cannonball is also the name of an X-Men superhero, a mutant who can fly as fast as a jet, while protected by an invisible force field.

PAIR WITH Prime rib, steak, venison or burgers.

UNCORK At barbecues; any party with pirates, sailors or X-Men fans. Or stick it in the cellar for a couple of years.

COLBY RED

Wine World Estates	Colby Red	
WINERY	WINE NAME	
Red blend (see below)	2009	
VARIETY	YEAR	
California, US	$16	
ORIGIN	PRICE	CLOSURE

Finally, a wine for every sweetheart who loves to drink wine and support a good cause. Before he turned 10 years old, Colby Rex Groom had undergone two open-heart surgeries. All went well, and these days he's a fine young man who wants to help others with similar health issues.

He paired up with his father to create Colby Red, an easygoing red blend (Cabernet Sauvignon, Zinfandel, Shiraz, Merlot and Petite Sirah) with mild tannins, lots of fruit and vanilla notes. All sales go toward charities that promote heart health.

TRIVIA Until 1990, before moving to California, winemaker Daryl Groom—Colby's dad—was the red wine maker at Australia's legendary Penfolds. He oversaw production of Penfolds Grange, one of the world's most iconic wines.

PAIR WITH Homemade burgers, roast chicken, steak, sausages, roast beef, stew. Anything hearty. Get it?

UNCORK Valentine's Day, any time in February (heart health month), any time you feel like a good glass of wine and supporting a fine cause.

THE DREAMING TREE

The Dreaming Tree	Crush	
WINERY	WINE NAME	
Merlot/Zinfandel	2009	
VARIETY	YEAR	
North Coast, California, US	$25	
ORIGIN	PRICE	CLOSURE

One for fans of Dave Matthews. Yeah, the musician. He's not a winemaker but he is a huge wine buff and, lucky for us, teamed up with a real winemaker (a fellow named Steve Reeder) to lend his moniker to a line of California wines. Crush is an easygoing blend of Merlot and Zinfandel, and the name Dreaming Tree comes from a song by Matthews, found on his 1998 album, *Before These Crowded Streets*.

TRIVIA Matthews isn't the first celeb to lend his moniker to a wine label. Others include the Rolling Stones, AC/DC, Pink Floyd, Deep Purple, actress Drew Barrymore, fashion designer Roberto Cavalli, Dr. Ruth Westheimer and socialite Paris Hilton. Oh, and Hello Kitty. Can't forget Hello Kitty.

PAIR WITH Ribs, Mediterranean grilled vegetables, burgers, pizza.

UNCORK While listening to Dave Matthews songs, of course, on picnics, while camping, at outdoor jam sessions.

EVOLUTION RED

Sokol Blosser	Evolution Red	
WINERY	WINE NAME	
Organic red blend (see below)	Non-vintage	
VARIETY	YEAR	
Oregon, US	$24	
ORIGIN	PRICE	CLOSURE

Sokol Blosser is a family-owned winery that has been organic ever since it was created in 1971. The family used to make a lovely red blend called Meditrina, but are now phasing it out and replacing it with Evolution Red, a new blend that's just as delicious. The winery's fans (there are many of us) will also likely notice the new vino is a partner to the winery's popular Evolution White. This one's a Syrah-based blend, and although no one's telling exactly what it's in it, I'm guessing there's some Pinot Noir, too, because the winery specializes in Pinot Noir. But maybe I'm wrong. Either way, it's yum—fruity, well-balanced, smooth.

TRIVIA In 1971, Tom Jones had a hit with "She's a Lady," Charles Manson was convicted of murder and locked up for life, Walt Disney World opened in Florida, and John Lennon released his song "Imagine."

PAIR WITH Homemade burgers, gourmet flatbread pizza, barbecued chicken, lasagna.

UNCORK Earth Day, Earth Hour, Friday nights with long-time friends, any time you feel like starting an Evolution.

LOUIS M. MARTINI

Louis M. Martini
WINERY

Cabernet Sauvignon — 2009
VARIETY — YEAR

Sonoma County, California, US — $20
ORIGIN — PRICE — CLOSURE

Winemaker Michael Martini is the third generation of his family to be making great wine in California. These days, he focuses almost entirely on Cabernet Sauvignon and, in the process, has become a bit of a legend for his mastery of the grape. This rich, full-bodied red features all the plum and blackberry notes you'd expect from a good Cabernet, wrapped up in a smooth-as-silk package. Wine geeks will want to know it's made from a blend of grapes grown on various top sites throughout Sonoma County, but the winery also has several prestigious vineyards in Napa Valley.

TRIVIA In 1899, Louis M. Martini—Michael's grandfather—moved from Genoa, Italy, to California when he was 12 years old, following his father who had moved to the country earlier. In 1933, he opened the winery that still bears his name.

PAIR WITH A big slab of beef, bison or slow-roasted lamb, hard aged cheese. Or just enjoy by itself. I did.

UNCORK Tonight, tomorrow, any night this week, month or year. Or cellar for another year or two or three. Only share with special friends or white wine fans (more for you, and that's a bonus).

MCMANIS FAMILY VINEYARDS

McManis Family Vineyards
WINERY

Petite Sirah — VARIETY
2010 — YEAR

Northern California, US — ORIGIN
$19 — PRICE
CLOSURE

Oh, my. This Petite Sirah is so dark and lovely, so savoury and chewy, with hints of vanilla and cocoa. What's not to love? It's a meal in a glass, from a family that's been in the business for a long time. The McManis family has been farming (and growing grapes) in northern California for generations, since 1938, and made the move to create a winery in 1990.

TRIVIA Petite Sirah is also known as Durif. François Durif, a French botanist, discovered it in 1880 and subsequently named the grape after himself. A modest fellow, he was.

PAIR WITH Slow-roasted meats, or just enjoy it by itself. And, if you're one of those people who loves the idea of pairing red wine with chocolate, this is your wine.

UNCORK Campfires, gourmet barbecues, romantic nights.

MÉLANGE NOIR

Waterbrook WINERY	Mélange Noir WINE NAME	
Red blend (see below) VARIETY	2009 YEAR	
Columbia Valley, Washington, US ORIGIN	$18 PRICE	CLOSURE

This wine appeared in the 2010 edition of *Uncorked!* Located in the heart of Walla Walla, Washington (say that 10 times fast), Waterbrook was the fourth winery registered in the region. Now there are more than a hundred, and Waterbrook is still thriving.

Why? The wine says it all. This super-easy red is soft and smooth, a blend of about 16 different types of grapes, including Merlot, Cabernet Sauvignon, Sangiovese, Cabernet Franc and Petit Verdot.

TRIVIA One of the definitions of the First Nations term Walla Walla is "running water," which is how Waterbrook got its name.

PAIR WITH Steak, shawarma, roast beef, pork loin, lamb, turkey.

UNCORK Now, at large family gatherings; any time someone says, "Bring a red," but doesn't tell you what they're serving; any time you just want a glass of reliably good red wine.

PAUL DOLAN

Paul Dolan Vineyards
WINERY

Organic Zinfandel — VARIETY
2009 — YEAR

California, US — ORIGIN
$22 — PRICE
CLOSURE

Wild turkeys wander through fields of blooming mustard, planted between the rows of the biodynamic vineyards at Paul Dolan's winery. It's that kind of place—a place where people, plants and animals can all just hang out and groove, according to the earth, the sun and the moon, not according to a corporate schedule. That sort of life results in some lip-smacking good Zinfandel, too. Pepper, jam and berry notes abound.

TRIVIA Check out the biodynamic phases of the moon calendar at pauldolanwine.com. It'll tell you the best days of the week to drink wine, too.

PAIR WITH Smoky ribs, ratatouille, pasta with tomato sauce.

UNCORK Earth Day, Earth Hour, any time you want a big ol' California red that'll knock your socks off and be good to you and the earth, too.

PEACHY CANYON

Peachy Canyon
WINERY

Petite Sirah	2009	
VARIETY	YEAR	
Paso Robles, California, US	$24	
ORIGIN	PRICE	CLOSURE

Dark and mysterious, Petite Sirah is the biker dude of wine grapes. If it were an astrological sign, it would be a Scorpio. You get the picture. It's tough, but you're sort of drawn to it just the same because you know it's complex. It's fascinating. And it is, in its own way, rather sexy.

And sometimes, just sometimes, it's very surprising. Take this one, for instance. Started by a couple of teachers in search of a better life, Peachy Canyon isn't exactly a tough-guy winery name, so maybe that's why this Petite Sirah is so kind and gentle. Expect a super-dark red wine with notes of cocoa, vanilla and juicy dark fruits. And smooth tannins. Very smooth.

TRIVIA Petite Sirah is primarily grown in California and Australia, where it is generally referred to by its alter ego, Durif.

PAIR WITH Red meats, especially a thick grilled steak. Or just enjoy it on its own.

UNCORK Backyard barbecues, Sunday dinners, book club gatherings, chick nights.

RAVENSWOOD

WINERY	WINE NAME	
Ravenswood	Vintners Blend	

VARIETY	YEAR	
Zinfandel	2009	

ORIGIN	PRICE	CLOSURE
Sonoma, California, US	$20	

This wine appeared in the 2010 edition of *Uncorked!* The Ravenswood winery specializes in Zinfandel, so it stands to reason that the winemaking team would do a good job of it. Although they make several different types, this entry-level (aka one of the most affordable) Zin is always reliable, interesting and tasty. The wine is made from grapes grown on gnarly, twisted, ancient old vines; those old vines apparently help the grapes to concentrate their flavour, so they offer more to wine lovers than grapes grown on young vines. Joel Peterson—who started the winery in 1976—gave Ravenswood its slogan: "No wimpy wines." You'll know why once you try this brash baby.

TRIVIA In 1976, CW McCall had a hit with the song "Convoy," Sonny and Cher got divorced, and the comedy series *Laverne and Shirley* premiered on TV.

PAIR WITH Barbecued ribs, lamb, Italian sausages.

UNCORK Swinging '70s parties, tailgate parties, backyard barbecues, any time you "got a great big convoy, rockin' through the night."

SHORTHORN CANYON

Wente Vineyards	Shorthorn Canyon	
WINERY	WINE NAME	
Syrah	2008	
VARIETY	YEAR	
Livermore Valley, California, US	$16	
ORIGIN	PRICE	CLOSURE

At more than 129 years in business, Wente is the oldest continuously operated family winery in the US. During Prohibition, the family kept the winery going by making sacramental wine for church services. The Shorthorn Canyon name is a nod to the cattle the family raised during that time. Made from estate-grown grapes, this smooth-as-silk Syrah is a real winner, with spicy notes of cherry, cranberry and vanilla.

TRIVIA When fifth-generation winemaker Karl Wente isn't making wine or tootling around the vineyards on his motorcycle, he also finds time to play guitar in The Front Porch Band.

PAIR WITH A nice steak (my apologies to shorthorn cattle everywhere).

UNCORK Now, rodeos, branding season, barbecues, big family gatherings.

THE SHOW

Three Thieves	The Show	
WINERY	WINE NAME	
Cabernet Sauvignon	2010	
VARIETY	YEAR	
Napa Valley, California, US	$19	
ORIGIN	PRICE	CLOSURE

C'mon. You knew when you saw this label that it would have to be in a bargain wine book for a province that hosts the Calgary Stampede, didn't you? This bottle is more than just a groovy package, however; it's rockin' good wine, too. The Show is a creation of three very talented winemakers—Charles Beiler, Joel Gott and Roger Scommegna (aka "Scommes" to his friends)—who started their collaboration in 2002.

As for the wine, it's a beautiful example of California Cab, albeit, at a price that won't make you beg for mercy. It's not jammy, but, as the name implies, it's showy, with just a hint of that sweetness that many newbie wine drinkers love. Look for vanilla, chocolate and blackberries, all wrapped up in a big, sexy, red package.

TRIVIA The label is both created and inspired by Hatch Show Print, an American design firm that was started in the late 1800s and created now-legendary posters for The Grand Ol' Opry, Hank Williams, Johnny Cash and many more.

PAIR WITH Steak, barbecue, game.

UNCORK Rodeos, tailgate parties, Stampede, alt-country jam sessions.

SIX EIGHT NINE

689 Cellars
WINERY

Red blend (see below) 2010
VARIETY YEAR

Napa Valley, California, US $25
ORIGIN PRICE CLOSURE

There is, of course, a great story behind the name of this wine. Behind this smooth-as-silk red are friends who love travelling to China and the surrounding countries—and they love Chinese culture, too. In Chinese numerology, the numbers six, eight and nine represent happiness, wealth and longevity, respectively. As for the wine, it's a lush, jammy, crowd-pleasing mishmash of grapes, including Zinfandel, Syrah, Cabernet Sauvignon, Merlot and Petit Sirah.

TRIVIA St. Augustine of Hippo apparently once said that "numbers are the universal language offered by the deity to humans as confirmation of the truth." Truth is, this wine's delicious.

PAIR WITH Grilled meats of all kinds, or just enjoy by itself.

UNCORK Any time you need a bit of luck or need to share some luck with someone else, big family gatherings, New Year's Eve, New Year's Day; any time someone says, "Bring a red," but doesn't tell you what they're making.

STONE CELLARS

Beringer Vineyards	Stone Cellars by Beringer	
WINERY	WINE NAME	
Merlot	2010	
VARIETY	YEAR	
California, US	$14	
ORIGIN	PRICE	CLOSURE

The name Stone Cellars is in honour of the original Beringer winery, a large stone building—depicted on the label—built in 1876.

Consistently good from year to year, this easy-drinking red is 90 percent Merlot, with a touch of Cabernet Sauvignon and Petite Sirah tossed in for extra body, colour and complexity.

TRIVIA A protected oak tree on the Beringer estate called the Leaning Oak is now more than 200 years old. It was alive when the Constitution of the United States of America was signed in 1787.

PAIR WITH Chili, pasta with red sauce, lasagna, lamb, burgers, pizza. Or just enjoy by itself.

UNCORK Mid-week pick-me-ups, tailgate parties, Friday movie nights with friends, any time you're just hanging out and want a friendly, über-affordable red to sip.

TRIBUNAL

Tribunal Cellars Winery
WINERY

Red blend (see below) — VARIETY
2009 — YEAR

Sonoma County, California, US — ORIGIN
$20 — PRICE
CLOSURE

Finally, a wine for mystery fans. This red is a blend of about nine different grapes, but exactly what, well, that's a secret. And the winery may or may not really exist; no one seems to know much, and those who do know more, aren't talking. What we do know is that it started its life as a product of Trader Joe's, a rather eccentric American grocery store chain that's made a reputation for yummy food products (and booze) at tasty deals. This crowd-pleaser is a prime example; it's delicious, with big—but not too big—notes of vanilla, cherry, chocolate and a hint of mint. As for the label, it's a woodcut courtroom scene, with dressed-up animals weighing in a wine. The judge? A cat.

TRIVIA Trader Joe's is also the home of Charles Shaw wines, perhaps best known as "Two-Buck Chuck" because, when it was released, it literally retailed for two bucks in the US. Now, why can't we get that Trader Joe's wine in Canada, I want to know?

PAIR WITH Steak, gourmet burgers, roast lamb, grilled vegetables. Or just enjoy by itself.

UNCORK Weekend dinners with friends, family barbecues, watching *Law & Order* reruns, reading mystery novels on the sofa.

WRITER'S BLOCK

Steele Wines	Writer's Block	
WINERY	WINE NAME	
Counoise	2010	
VARIETY	YEAR	
Lake County, California, US	$21	
ORIGIN	PRICE	CLOSURE

If you drink wine, you've seen some interesting labels. This may be one of them. I'm not talking about the painting on the front, which may or may not be William Shakespeare. I'm talking about the back: an eccentric, rambling, vaguely poetic monologue about wine and life, stuff like "Normally words trip off my tongue like hundreds of curbside drunks trying to hail the same taxicab."

The wine inside—made from Counoise, a relatively uncommon French grape—is also interesting. Expect an aromatic red, with soft tannins and notes of toast, cinnamon and cherries.

TRIVIA Jed Steele has been in the winemaking business in California for close to 45 years. He helped start Kendall-Jackson Wine Estates and spent 10 years there before starting Steele Wines.

PAIR WITH Beef Bourguignon. Or cellar for a couple of years.

UNCORK With writers, wine lovers, lovers. Or just enjoy it by itself.

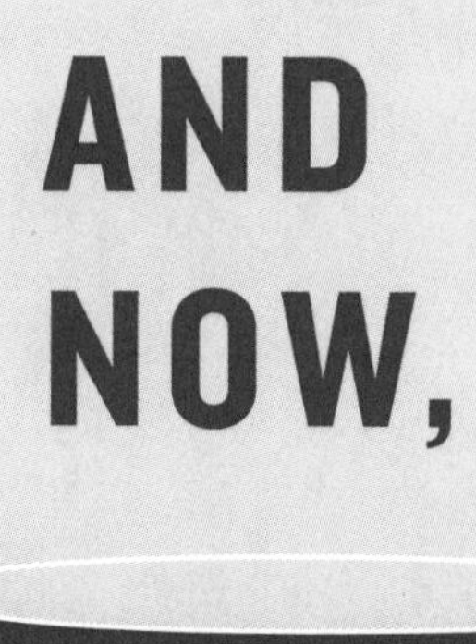

THE WHITE WINES

CHOOK RAFFLE

Shoofly Wines	Chook Raffle	
WINERY	WINE NAME	
Chardonnay/Riesling/Verdelho	2011	
VARIETY	YEAR	
Adelaide Hills, Australia	$18	
ORIGIN	PRICE	CLOSURE

How can you resist a wine that sounds like a secret code, a slightly uncomfortable cross between a church fundraiser and what you do on a hot, sticky summer day?

I'd want to be drinking a wine like this on a hot, sticky summer day. This fragrant white—mostly Chardonnay, with a hint of Riesling and Verdelho—is filled with zing and citrus. It is full bodied and fun, with notes of tropical fruit, a touch of spice and bucketfuls of moxie. Ben Riggs is the winemaker here; he's a hotshot young Australian winemaker who's making his mark throughout the country's top wine regions.

TRIVIA A chook is Aussie slang for a chicken. The term "chook raffle" refers to an Australian tradition, where a chicken or chicken meat is raffled off as a fundraiser. Nowadays it also refers to people who think they're organized but aren't—in other words, "They couldn't even run a chook raffle."

PAIR WITH Roast chook (apologies to the bird), mild seafood. Serve chilled.

UNCORK Hoedowns, barn dances, patio parties, any time the Shoofly fits.

FIFTH LEG

Devil's Lair	Fifth Lair	
WINERY	WINE NAME	
Sémillon/Sauvignon Blanc	2012	
VARIETY	YEAR	
Margaret River, Western Australia	$16	
ORIGIN	PRICE	CLOSURE

If you ever find yourself in Margaret River, make the time for surfing, whale-watching and, of course, drinking wine. Grapes for making wine have only been grown in Australia's Margaret River for about 40 years, but the region's winemakers have been quickly creating a name for themselves, primarily for crisp, fragrant whites such as this one. It is as mouth-watering as a roll of SweeTarts, and a heck of a lot more grown up. Expect a taste explosion of floral, honeydew melon, lime and kiwi notes.

TRIVIA The name Fifth Leg comes from a famous Australian archaeological site, Devil's Lair. Located close to the winery, the cave is famous for the 50,000-year-old fossilized remains of a Tasmanian tiger—with a mysterious fifth leg found in its midst. Why? No one knows.

And the dog on the label is partly in homage to the fact that Devil's Lair winery, where the Fifth Leg wines are made, always has a resident winery dog or two, who love attention from visitors.

PAIR WITH Spicy Asian dishes, salads, simply prepared white fish and scallop dishes, fresh oysters, roast chicken. Serve chilled.

UNCORK Picnics, Sunday afternoons on the patio, the dog days of summer.

TAHBILK

Tahbilk
WINERY

Marsanne	2009	
VARIETY	YEAR	
Nagambie Lakes, Australia	$20	
ORIGIN	PRICE	CLOSURE

Tahbilk is one of Australia's oldest wineries, and still has some Shiraz vines that date back to that time. Indeed, some of the Marsanne vines used to make this very wine date back to 1927—perhaps not quite to the winery's start in 1860, but still, you get the picture. They're rather elderly.

One for fans of Chardonnay to seek out, Marsanne is a white wine grape that's especially common in France's Rhône Valley. It also does beautifully in Australia, as this classy example proves. Creamy and spicy, it has notes of peach and grapefruit.

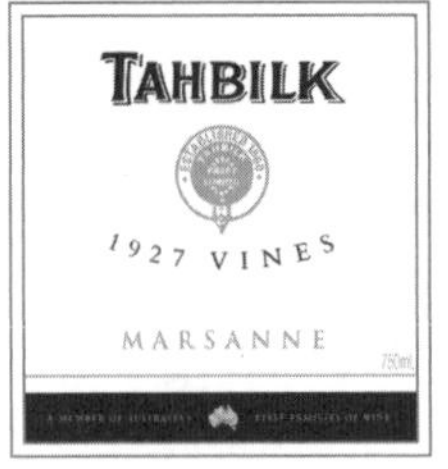

TRIVIA Nagambie Lakes, by the way, is located about 120 kilometres north of Melbourne. One of Australia's most famous characters, Ned Kelly, hailed from the region. Some refer to him as a hero. Others call him an outlaw. Either way, the man's short, violent life is still the stuff of books and movies, more than 100 years after his death.

PAIR WITH Seafood, sushi, halibut, breaded fish and chips. Serve chilled.

UNCORK With gangsters, old-timers, history buffs and Chardonnay fans.

WISHING CLOCK OF THE ADELAIDE HILLS

Dandelion Vineyards WINERY	Wishing Clock of the Adelaide Hills WINE NAME	
Sauvignon Blanc VARIETY	2011 YEAR	
Adelaide Hills, Australia ORIGIN	$22 PRICE	CLOSURE

Poet laureates, schmoet laureates. I love poetry, but really, we need some sort of wine laureate, and I vote for this one, in honour of Alberta's unofficial flower (apologies to our wild rose). There's even a Canuck connection to this faraway winery—former Calgarian Brad Rey, one of Dandelion's principals (aka important dudes), lives in Australia but still sometimes comes back to Calgary.

The folks at Dandelion get their grapes from several of Australia's top wine-producing regions, including Eden Valley, McLaren Vale, the Barossa Valley and Adelaide Hills, where this zingy Sauvignon Blanc comes from. It's crisp and saucy, with grassy, herbal, mineral and citrus notes. And, of course, there's a fluffy drawing of a dandelion on the label. I'm warning you, though—if you try Dandelion wines, you may forget that those little yellow flowers are actually pests.

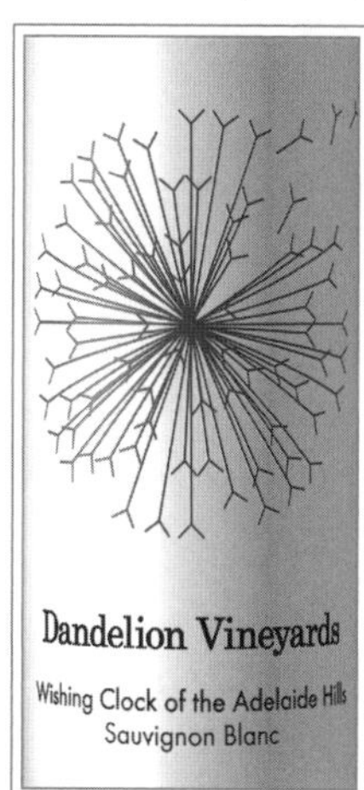

TRIVIA Dandelion leaves contain vitamins D, A, C and B, as well as zinc, potassium and iron. They can be served in salads, and the flowers can be made into jelly. I know. My French teacher had us make the jelly in Grade 7. I got an A.

PAIR WITH Salads, fresh asparagus, simple seafood dishes. Serve chilled.

UNCORK With farmers, locavores, foodies and loyal Calgarians who still dream of faraway places.

RABL

Weingut Rudolf Rabl	Rabl
WINERY	WINE NAME
Grüner Veltliner	2010
VARIETY	YEAR
Kamptal, Austria	$20
ORIGIN	PRICE

CLOSURE

This wine appeared in the 2010 edition of *Uncorked!* The Rabl family, who own this winery, have been farming on this estate since 1750. In fact, their cellar was built at least 300 years ago. And, like the Rabl family, Grüner Veltliner wines go back a long, long way in Austrian history; they're considered to be the nation's signature white wines. Throughout history, winemakers have tweaked their formulations to keep up with the times. This modern, very dry white wine is a fine example.

TRIVIA *Weingut* is the German word for winery. And the name Spiegel, on the label, refers to the vineyard where these grapes were grown.

PAIR WITH Roast ham, Chinese food, Asian fusion dishes, crab cakes, asparagus, artichokes, roast pork with applesauce. Serve chilled.

UNCORK Easter, book club, mid-week takeout.

VELTLINSKY

Graf Hardegg	Veltlinsky	
WINERY	WINE NAME	
Grüner Veltliner	2009	
VARIETY	YEAR	
Seefeld-Kadolz, Austria	$20	
ORIGIN	PRICE	CLOSURE

Wine production here dates back to the 1600s and, some say, much earlier. Graf Hardegg is perhaps best known by Austrian wine purists for fancy, serious wines, but the Veltlinsky label is anything but. Fun, unpretentious and downright delicious, this wine is made from 100 percent Grüner Veltliner, pronounced *GROON-er Velt-LEEN-er*. It's dry and fresh, with notes of green apple and spice, and not too much acidity.

TRIVIA Graf Hardegg is located north of Vienna, on the northern edge of Austria's largest wine region, Weinviertel, a word that literally translates as "the wine district." Makes sense, I'm thinking.

PAIR WITH Scallops, white fish, creamy mild white cheeses. Serve chilled.

UNCORK Now, with groovy friends and/or members of the Arnold Schwarzenegger fan club (including the man himself. He's from Austria, in case you've forgotten.)

CALLIOPE

Burrowing Owl Estate Winery	Calliope	
WINERY	WINE NAME	
Sauvignon Blanc	2010	
VARIETY	YEAR	
Okanagan Valley, BC, Canada	$18	
ORIGIN	PRICE	CLOSURE

Located on Black Sage Road in the Okanagan Valley, Burrowing Owl has long been one of the most consistent, serious wineries in the country. But this offshoot label gives its winemaking team a place where they can be creative and play at work, where they can try out new projects and simply have some fun. This crisp, citrusy white is 100 percent Sauvignon Blanc and 100 percent fun.

TRIVIA The Calliope wines are named after the Calliope hummingbird, Canada's smallest bird. Calliope means "beautiful voice."

PAIR WITH Salads, asparagus, Asian takeout, roast turkey or chicken. Serve chilled.

UNCORK Now, with good friends, during patio season.

CEDARCREEK PROPRIETOR'S WHITE

CedarCreek Estate Winery	Proprietor's White	
WINERY	WINE NAME	
White blend (see below)	2011	
VARIETY	YEAR	
Okanagan Valley, BC, Canada	$13	
ORIGIN	PRICE	CLOSURE

This wine appeared in the 2010 edition of *Uncorked!* One of the first eight wineries in the Okanagan, CedarCreek was started by Senator Ross Fitzpatrick (now retired). Born and raised in the Okanagan Valley, he went on to achieve fame and fortune in the rest of the province, but never forgot his family roots.

The winery makes a range of fine wines, but this one is value priced and made to please every white wine fan; it's a creative blend of Chardonnay, Pinot Blanc, Ehrenfelser, Gewurztraminer and Riesling. With that in mind, expect a simple, tasty wine with fragrant, fruity, crisp notes.

TRIVIA Ehrenfelser is a cross between Riesling and Sylvaner grapes. It was developed in 1929 in Germany but it's especially popular in the Okanagan Valley, partly because it can handle BC's winter temperatures.

PAIR WITH Roast chicken or turkey, spicy Asian curries. Or serve by itself before dinner.

UNCORK Canada Day, budget-conscious dinners, any time you're asked to bring a white wine, but nobody tells you what's on the menu.

GENERATION SEVEN

Château des Charmes	Generation Seven	
WINERY	WINE NAME	
White blend (see below)	2010	
VARIETY	YEAR	
Niagara-on-the-Lake, Canada	$18	
ORIGIN	PRICE	CLOSURE

A blend of Riesling, Gewürztraminer and Sauvignon Blanc, this fresh, crisp, off-dry, unoaked white is the secondary (also known as the less expensive and more fun) label from one of Niagara's most-established wineries, Château des Charmes.

The Bosc family—who own Château des Charmes—have been making wine for seven generations, hence the name. They've made wine on three continents—Africa, Europe and North America.

TRIVIA A portion of the proceeds from every bottle of Generation Seven goes to Meal Exchange, a Canadian charity that endeavours to feed hungry kids.

PAIR WITH Roast chicken, spicy Asian curries, shawarma, salads. Serve chilled.

UNCORK On the patio, family gatherings, Mom's birthday.

MT. BOUCHERIE

Mt. Boucherie Family Estate Winery

WINERY

Pinot Gris	2011	
VARIETY	YEAR	
Okanagan Valley, BC, Canada	$23	
ORIGIN	PRICE	CLOSURE

The Gidda family moved to the Okanagan Valley from India in the late 1960s, and they grew grapes for many years before opening the winery just over 10 years ago. Since then, they've carved out a reputation for fair-priced and reliable wines such as this lush, lovely Pinot Gris. No wallflower, this wine—it's loaded with peachy, spicy flavours that leave you wanting more. And more. And more.

TRIVIA The winery is named after the mountain of the same name in West Kelowna, which overlooks the winery's vineyard from the west. As for the mountain, it's named after Isadore Boucherie, one of the region's early settlers who lived in the 1800s.

PAIR WITH Salmon, roast chicken or turkey, pork loin, Chinese or Indian takeout. Serve chilled.

UNCORK Canada Day, chick-flick nights, Thanksgiving, Christmas, summer afternoons on the patio.

7 BLANC

Township 7 Vineyards & Winery	7 Blanc	
WINERY	WINE NAME	
White blend (see below)	2011	
VARIETY	YEAR	
Okanagan Valley, BC, Canada	$16	
ORIGIN	PRICE	CLOSURE

Technically, Township 7 has two locations—the original opened in Langley in 2001, and a second winery, located on the Naramata Bench in the Okanagan Valley, was added two years later. All of the grapes for this über-fragrant wine—a blend of Pinot Gris, Gewürztraminer and Muscat—were grown at Naramata. Perhaps a sign of what it's made from, it's a mishmash of tasty flavours—grapefruit and pear, peach and lemon, flowers and spice. If this wine were a puppy, it would be the loveable mutt you'd refuse to leave behind.

TRIVIA The winery gets its name from the history of South Langley near Vancouver. In the late 1800s, the community was known as Township 7.

PAIR WITH Sushi, Thai green curry, Indian takeout, goat cheese flatbread. Serve chilled.

UNCORK Friday nights, weekend picnics, Sunday afternoon lunches.

SIBLING RIVALRY

Henry of Pelham	Sibling Rivalry	
WINERY	WINE NAME	
White blend (see below)	2011	
VARIETY	YEAR	
Niagara Peninsula, Canada	$18	
ORIGIN	PRICE	CLOSURE

This wine appeared in the 2010 edition of *Uncorked!* What happens when three brothers work together? Sometimes they fight. Doesn't matter how much they love each other. When Paul, Daniel and Matthew Speck—owners of Henry of Pelham, one of Niagara's top wineries—scrap, they figure out creative ways to work out their issues. One way? Making wine. This crisp, super-fragrant white wine is made from a combination of Riesling, Chardonnay and Gewürztraminer grapes—a variety for each brother. Don't miss the top of the screwcap, which features three sets of hands playing Rock, Paper, Scissors.

TRIVIA The Specks' great-great-great-grandfather Nicholas Smith farmed on the winery's land in 1794. His youngest son built the building that is now the winery. His name? Henry. And the winery's address? Pelham Road.

PAIR WITH Shrimp masala, green Thai and coconut milk curries, pad Thai, Vietnamese subs. Or just drink by itself. Serve chilled.

UNCORK Now, with your siblings (if they have a sense of humour), on sunny patio days, mid-week meals.

SUMAC RIDGE

Sumac Ridge Estate Winery	Private Reserve	
WINERY	WINE NAME	
Gewürztraminer	2011	
VARIETY	YEAR	
Okanagan Valley, BC, Canada	$15	
ORIGIN	PRICE	CLOSURE

One of the oldest wineries in British Columbia, Sumac Ridge was started by Canadian wine legend Harry McWatters. Although Harry has since moved on to other wine projects, the folks at Sumac Ridge still make all kinds of wonderful wines—and the Gewürztraminer is always a standout.

Pronounced *Guh-VYRTS-trah-mee-nuhr*, this wine smells like roses, lychee and spice, with a hint of grapefruit. Probably related to the Pinot family of grapes (Pinot Noir, Pinot Gris), it first showed up in Germany more than 1,000 years ago.

TRIVIA The German word *Gewürz* literally translates as "spicy" in English.

PAIR WITH Turkey, grilled white fish, Chinese food, blue cheese. Or just enjoy by itself. Serve chilled.

UNCORK Family gatherings, turkey days, casual Fridays.

SUMMERHILL EHRENFELSER

Summerhill Pyramid Winery
WINERY

Organic Ehrenfelser | 2011
VARIETY | YEAR

Okanagan Valley, BC, Canada | $24
ORIGIN | PRICE | CLOSURE

Summerhill is surely one of the most interesting and unusual wineries in Canada, if not North America. First, there's the estate's pyramid, a massive structure modelled after the Great Pyramid in Egypt, where all of its multiple award-winning wines are aged. Then there's the fact that all of those wines are also organic and biodynamic, meaning they've been made with minimal intervention following the ideas of Rudolph Steiner, an Austrian philosopher who lived in the 1920s.

As for this particular wine, it's made from Ehrenfelser, a grape with roots—pardon the pun—in Germany. Pronounced *AIR-ren-fel-zer*, this versatile, fragrant white has notes of honeysuckle, orange blossom and melon. The 2011 vintage marks the 20th anniversary of this wine.

TRIVIA Egypt's Great Pyramid is made with about 2.3 million stone blocks, each weighing 2.5 to 15 tons.

PAIR WITH Roast chicken or turkey, mildly spiced vegetarian dishes, pork loin. Or enjoy by itself. Serve chilled.

UNCORK Now, Canada Day, Thanksgiving, Christmas, any time you need an easy-drinking white wine.

CONO SUR

Cono Sur
WINERY

Organic Chardonnay — 2011
VARIETY — YEAR

Valle de San Antonio, Chile — $14
ORIGIN — PRICE — CLOSURE

Although Cono Sur was created around Chile's oldest Pinot Noir vines, it also makes wonderful whites, including this lively organic Chardonnay. Indeed, the bicycle on this label stands for the winery's environmental commitment—it was the world's first carbon-neutral winery, and in the fields, workers pedal from row to row on bicycle. But back to the wine for a minute; it's refreshing and citrusy, with just a kiss of richness from a wee bit of time in oak.

TRIVIA Looking for great pairing suggestions and recipes? Go to conosur.com and click on the "virtual sommelier" in the top right corner.

PAIR WITH Sushi, salmon, roast chicken or turkey. Serve chilled.

UNCORK Casual Fridays with friends, picnics, patio days, turkey days.

LE BEL ANGE

Domaine Begude	Le Bel Ange	
WINERY	WINE NAME	
Organic Chardonnay/Chenin Blanc		2011
VARIETY		YEAR
Languedoc-Roussillon, France	$20	
ORIGIN	PRICE	CLOSURE

I can't resist a wine with a name that, translated into English, means "the beautiful angel." This wine—an unoaked Chardonnay with some Chenin Blanc thrown in—comes from a small family-owned winery that has been farmed organically for more than 30 years. (Wine has been made on the estate since the 1500s.) The couple that currently owns the estate relocated from London, England, almost 10 years ago, after tiring of the hustle and bustle of big-city life. The wine is named in honour of their young daughter, Millie, who was born shortly after they made the big move. As for the Bel Ange, it is just as lovely as its name, with lots of fine mineral, citrus and apple notes.

TRIVIA The Occitan language was spoken in ancient Languedoc, and although it isn't recognized as an official language it is still used by about 500,000 people in France.

PAIR WITH Seafood, salads, roast chicken or roast turkey. Serve chilled.

UNCORK Christmas, Thanksgiving, first dates, third dates, anniversaries, any occasion when you need to remind someone they're beautiful.

PAUL ZINCK

Paul Zinck
WINERY

Pinot Blanc — VARIETY
2010 — YEAR

Alsace, France — ORIGIN
$18 — PRICE
CLOSURE

The father-son team behind Paul Zinck has, for many years, been creating a range of beautiful wines that thrill critics and ordinary wine drinkers alike.

This Pinot Blanc manages to be mysterious, minerally, fruity, herbal, smoky—and yet, still dry, crisp and clean. Try it and you'll know what I mean. If it were a perfume, everyone would be asking what it was and where they could get it.

And don't miss the little sticker on the back of this label. It can be torn off and tucked into your wallet, so you can remember the wine name (and the winery website) the next time you're shopping.

TRIVIA You say Pinot Blanc, I say . . . Klevner? In Austria, the grape can be called Klevner or Weissburgunder. In Spain and Italy, it's known as Pinot Bianco. And in Serbia, you'll find it as Beli Burgundac.

PAIR WITH Delicate soft cheeses, white fish, creamy pasta dishes. Serve chilled.

UNCORK With Francophiles, wine geeks and Euro-snobs, Thanksgiving dinners, dinner parties, wedding showers.

PHEASANT'S TEARS

Pheasant's Tears		
WINERY		
Rkatsiteli	2010	
VARIETY	YEAR	
Kakheti, Georgia	$23	
ORIGIN	PRICE	CLOSURE

Once part of the Soviet Union, the Republic of Georgia borders the Black Sea to the west, Turkey to the south and Russia to the north. Pheasant's Tears is a small winery in Georgia's main wine-producing region. The winery is partly owned by an American artist, John Wurdeman, who moved to Georgia to paint, but then fell in love—with the country and a beautiful Georgian woman—and stayed.

Pronounced *Er-kat-si-TEL-ee*, this dry white wine—sometimes called "amber" because of its intense colour—has nutty, citrus and honey notes. It's unfiltered, which means it may look slightly cloudy in your glass. That's okay—it's supposed to look like that. Don't taste this wine expecting it to be like anything else you've ever had. It isn't.

TRIVIA Georgia boasts one of the world's oldest winemaking traditions—more than 8,000 years—and about 500 indigenous grape varieties. At Pheasant's Tears, the wines are "natural" wines, meaning they don't have any added preservatives or chemicals. They're made by letting the grapes—skins and all—sit for several months in *qvevris*, large terracotta clay vessels that are buried in the ground, and then lined with a thin layer of organic beeswax.

PAIR WITH Fried chicken, grilled meats, grilled vegetables, tzaziki, feta cheese, homemade flatbreads. Serve chilled.

UNCORK With wine geeks and history buffs, any time you wish you could afford to travel someplace exotic but can't.

FRITZ'S RIESLING

Gunderloch	Fritz's Riesling	
WINERY	WINE NAME	
Riesling	2010	
VARIETY	YEAR	
Rheinhessen, Germany	$16	
ORIGIN	PRICE	CLOSURE

Technically, Fritz is a cartoon guy created by Gunderloch's marketing team, a funny little man with wild eyebrows and a spiky beard. However, they freely admit that their inspiration is the winery's co-owner Fritz Hasselbach, a legendary (and bearded) winemaker.

The winery was started by Hasselbach's wife's great-great-grandfather in 1890, and it has been famous for its Rieslings for more than 100 years. But don't expect this lively, off-dry (meaning it's a little bit sweet) sipper to be old-fashioned. As the packaging will show, it's über-modern and über-zesty, with mineral, lemon and lime notes. Tasty and fun.

TRIVIA Rheinhessen is the largest wine region in Germany, and Riesling is the most commonly grown grape in Germany. It is traditionally packaged in tall, thin bottles without much of a "punt," the dimple indentation that's commonly found on other bottle bottoms.

PAIR WITH Ham, pulled pork, pork loin with applesauce, spicy Asian takeout, curries, Chinese food. Serve chilled.

UNCORK Now, casual Friday dinners with friends, Easter meals, turkey days, hot afternoons on the patio.

GRUEN

Gruen
WINERY

Riesling	2010	
VARIETY	YEAR	
Rheingau, Germany	$14	
ORIGIN	PRICE	CLOSURE

In German, *gruen* means "green." It's an apt word to describe this wine, whether it refers to the taste (young, off-dry and crisp, with notes of green apples and lime) or the packaging, described on the front label as "climate-neutral." What does that mean? Everything—bottles, grapes, production—must be produced in a way that leaves no harmful effect on the environment. While the wine may not be labelled organic, at least it's helping to reduce greenhouse gases—something to consider, seeing that wineries ship their creations all over the world.

TRIVIA The Rheingau is one of 13 official wine regions in Germany. About 80 percent of the wine in the region is made from Riesling.

PAIR WITH Spicy cuisine, sushi, white fish dishes, salads, shellfish, Chinese or Indian takeout, Thai green curries. Or just enjoy by itself. Serve chilled.

UNCORK Patio parties, casual Friday night dinners, mid-week takeout.

LINGENFELDER

Lingenfelder	Bird Label	
WINERY	WINE NAME	
Riesling	2010	
VARIETY	YEAR	
Pfalz, Germany	$16	
ORIGIN	PRICE	CLOSURE

This wine appeared in the 2010 edition of *Uncorked!* The Vineyard Creatures line of wines from Lingenfelder all feature, well, a vineyard creature: owl, hare, fish, fox and bee. They're all worth seeking out. But one of the easiest to find? The delicious, approachable Bird Label Riesling. It's semi-dry, very food friendly and remarkably approachable. Winemaker Rainer Lingenfelder's family has been making wine in the Pfalz—Germany's warmest, driest wine region—for 13 generations, since the early 1500s.

TRIVIA According to a good source I know, Rainer Lingenfelder has his photo taken with everyone he meets, so he can remember them if their paths cross again.

PAIR WITH Mild pork dishes, sushi, spicy Thai or Indian dishes, curries, Chinese food. Serve chilled.

UNCORK Grandma's birthday, Friday nights with friends, any time you want to celebrate spring.

GALIL MOUNTAIN VIOGNIER

Galil Mountain
WINERY

Viognier | 2010
VARIETY | YEAR

Upper Galilee, Israel | $17
ORIGIN | PRICE | CLOSURE

Galil Mountain is located on the Upper Galilee mountain range, a ridge of mountains on the Israeli border, looking out toward Lebanon. This full-bodied white, made from Viognier grapes, is loaded with lush floral, apricot and peach notes. (The importer describes it as a "voluptuous Viognier." I'd claim those words as mine, if I could.) With loads of fragrant apricot and peach notes, Viognier is a wine for Chardonnay fans who want to try something new and interesting.

And a bonus for anyone Jewish—this wine is both kosher and kosher for Passover. Serve chilled.

TRIVIA Wine has been made in Israel for more than 2,000 years. There are currently more than 150 wineries in the tiny country. (It is about 20,000 square kilometres, compared with Canada at about 10 million square kilometres.)

PAIR WITH Turkey, roast chicken, simple white fish dishes. Or just enjoy by itself. Serve chilled.

UNCORK Thanksgiving, Jewish holidays and celebrations.

ANSELMI

Anselmi	San Vicenzo	
WINERY	WINE NAME	
White blend (see below)	2010	
VARIETY	YEAR	
Veneto, Italy	$20	
ORIGIN	PRICE	CLOSURE

One of Italy's top white wine producers, Roberto Anselmi has been cranking out good juice since the mid-1970s. Although he's in the Soave region, he opted out of the traditional naming system and decided to march to the beat of his own drum. And how. This stylish vino is crisp and approachable, with notes of citrus, peaches, melon and Granny Smith apples. It's mostly made from Garganega, indigenous to Italy and the country's sixth-most-planted grape. A touch of Yellow Traminer and Incrocio Manzone round out the blend. No oak. Just a fruity, zippy, young wine.

TRIVIA In addition to being the name of the vineyard where these grapes come from, San Vincenzo is also the name of a couple of Catholic saints, one of whom was a former soldier who converted to Christianity and was martyred for refusing to take part in sacrifices for the Roman emperor in AD 286. Vincenzo means "winner."

PAIR WITH Roast chicken, lobster, white fish dishes, soft cheeses, salads or pesto. Very food friendly.

UNCORK With wine geeks, Italophiles, Sauvignon Blanc fans.

ANTHÌLIA

Donnafugata	Anthìlia	
WINERY	WINE NAME	
Catarratto/Ansonica	2011	
VARIETY	YEAR	
Sicily, Italy	$19	
ORIGIN	PRICE	CLOSURE

The winery—Donnafugata, literally the "fugitive woman"—is named after a Hapsburg queen who fled from Napoleon in 1807 and settled on the island of Sicily. As for the wine, Anthìlia (as well as other Donnafugata wines) is named after a character in a famous Italian novel, *The Leopard*, by Guiseppe Tomasi di Lampedusa.

As for this crisp, powerful white, it has fruity, herbal notes and is made primarily from Catarratto and Ansonica grapes, although, depending on the vintage, others may be added. It's a solid performer, however, year after year.

TRIVIA Sicilians drink less wine than any other Italian region, but Sicily has more vineyards than any other area in Italy. Just in case you ever find yourself in Sicily on November 11, be sure to check out the local Festa del Vino celebrations—literally, the festival of the wine.

PAIR WITH Fish dishes with couscous, shellfish, ratatouille, roast chicken. Serve chilled.

UNCORK Do-it-yourself wine festivals, any time you feel like heading on vacation to someplace hot and European but can't afford to go.

LAMBERTI

Lamberti	Santepietre	
WINERY	WINE NAME	
Pinot Grigio	2011	
VARIETY	YEAR	
Trentino, Alto Adige, Italy	$13	
ORIGIN	PRICE	CLOSURE

For the past couple of years, Pinot Grigio has been one of the hottest wine trends in North America. And why not? It's food friendly, easy to drink and fun.

This one—from a renowned Italian producer dating back to the 1960s—offers lots of bang for the buck, with honey, apple and citrus notes, plus plenty of big, full white wine flavours. I'd say plenty of "mouthfeel" but that's one of those pretentious wine words that drives me crazy. What you need to know is that this wine is good. Period.

TRIVIA The archaeological museum of Alto Adige is home to the Ice Man, a Stone Age mummy dating back more than 4,000 years. His corpse was found frozen in the ice of the region's mountains. Alas, without wine.

PAIR WITH White fish, roast chicken, pork chops. Or enjoy by itself as an aperitif. Serve chilled.

UNCORK Now, with good friends, casual Fridays, Sunday afternoons, patio days, while watching *Desperate Housewives*.

KATO

Kato
WINERY

Sauvignon Blanc — VARIETY
2011 — YEAR

Marlborough, New Zealand — ORIGIN
$16 — PRICE
CLOSURE

So fresh and herbal, it reminds me of a summer morning. I want to run through water sprinklers on a hot day, wearing the bikini I had when I was six—yellow gingham, with a daisy on the front.

But—let's face it—these days, I'd rather skip the purple Freezie and instead celebrate a day like that with a chilled glass of wine in my hand. And there's nothing like Kato to bring back those memories, but in a cool grown-up sort of way. Bikini optional.

Bonus points to Kato for not just serving up a great wine; the company also supports the Whale and Dolphin Conservation Society, a global non-profit.

TRIVIA The word *kato* means "harvest" in Maori, the indigenous language of New Zealand. As for the Kato logo on the label, it features three stylized whale tails.

PAIR WITH Asparagus, salads, shellfish, white fish. Serve chilled.

UNCORK Patio afternoons, dinner with the boss, winter days when you long for the scent of fresh-cut grass.

THE PEOPLE'S PINOT GRIS

Corner 50 Winery	The People's Pinot Gris	
WINERY	WINE NAME	
Pinot Gris	2010	
VARIETY	YEAR	
Hawkes Bay, New Zealand	$17	
ORIGIN	PRICE	CLOSURE

This collaboration between an artist (one Martin Poppelwell) and a winemaking team was created with the idea in mind that when you taste a great bottle of wine, you exclaim, "This wine is a work of art." Or something like that. And, according to the back of the bottle, "Artists express themselves through their work, and winemakers are no different. They use grapes and the land to express their creativity." Don't miss the fun back label, either. It features a pie-chart map with a handful of the French and English descriptors for the wine (aromatic, unctuous, *exotique*, etc.). Easy to drink, fairly full bodied, lots of fruity notes.

TRIVIA Just in case you think this wine is some artsy-fartsy deal, it's actually a Constellation Brands project, the world's largest wine corporation. Real people—just part of a really big company.

PAIR WITH "Real food" (according to the label), pasta with Parmesan cheese and parsley. Serve chilled.

UNCORK With "real people," picnics, late-night stargazing (constellations. Get it?).

SPY VALLEY

Spy Valley Wine
WINERY

Pinot Gris — VARIETY
2011 — YEAR

Marlborough, New Zealand — ORIGIN
$20 — PRICE
CLOSURE

The name Spy Valley comes from the fact that the winery is located near a real spy base—aka a "satellite communications monitoring base"—in Marlborough's Wairau Valley.

As for Pinot Gris, it's one of the world's trendiest whites these days, and if you're not already part of the fan club, you will be after you try this gorgeous wine. Expect loads of juicy tropical fruit, gentle spice and peach notes.

TRIVIA The folks at Spy Valley follow all sorts of eco-friendly practices (minimal sprays, mulching). As part of those practices, they recycle their glass on-site, crushing it into dust that is then "mixed with mulch and distributed below the grapevines to enhance light reflection into the vines."

PAIR WITH Very mildly spiced dishes, so the food won't overpower the loveliness of the wine. Or just enjoy it by itself. Serve chilled.

UNCORK James Bond movie nights, CSIS fan club meetings, any time you feel like Diana Rigg's character in *The Avengers*.

TWIN ISLANDS

Twin Islands
WINERY

Sauvignon Blanc — VARIETY
2010 — YEAR

Marlborough, New Zealand — ORIGIN
$19 — PRICE
CLOSURE

This zippy, zingy, zesty wine is so much fun—just what you want to be drinking on one of Alberta's precious hot summer days. Expect citrus and herbal notes, plenty of acidity and plenty of charm. Named after New Zealand's two main islands, this label was started in 1992 by the folks at Nautilus Estate, a New Zealand winery that makes fine—but more expensive—Sauvignon Blanc (and Pinot Noir, too).

TRIVIA In 1992, Nirvana frontman Kurt Cobain married singer Courtney Love. Prince Andrew and Sarah Ferguson split up. And Euro Disney opened outside Paris, France.

PAIR WITH Salads, asparagus, goat cheese tarts. Or just enjoy by itself. Serve chilled.

UNCORK Now, picnics, casual Saturday afternoon lunches.

LUIS PATO VINHAS VELHAS

Luis Pato	Vinhas Velhas	
WINERY	WINE NAME	
Bical/Cerceal/Secialinho	2010	
VARIETY	YEAR	
Bairrada, Portugal	$20	
ORIGIN	PRICE	CLOSURE

Luis Pato (yes, there's really someone with the name) took over his family's winery in the 1980s, and now one of his three daughters works alongside him as a winemaker in her own right. Sometimes called "the King of Bairrada" by his friends, he's a real champion of Portuguese wines and of his country's fine array of indigenous grapes.

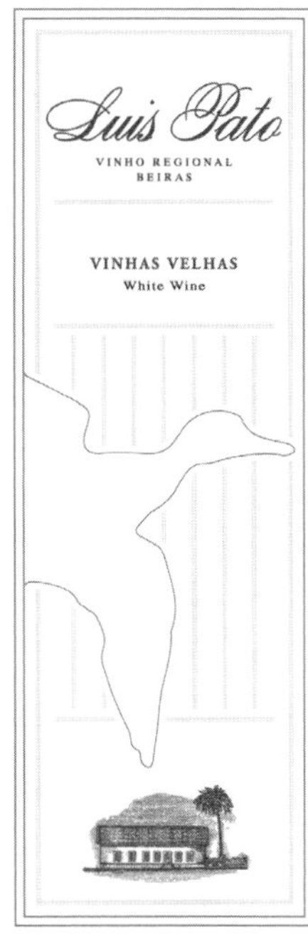

Not surprisingly, then, this aromatic sipper is a blend of indigenous white grapes called Bical, Cerceal and Secialinho. Just find the wine, taste it and look for fruity, lemony notes with a hint of buttered toast. One for fans of lightly oaked Chardonnay.

TRIVIA The word *pato* is Portuguese for "duck" (as in "quack, quack"), which explains the silhouette of the quacker on the label.

PAIR WITH Seafood, roast chicken, roast turkey, mildly seasoned roast duck (my apologies to *patos* everywhere), niçoise salad. Serve chilled.

UNCORK Picnics, hot afternoons on the patio, with wine geeks (they'll appreciate the unusual grape varieties).

PROVA RÉGIA

Quinta da Romeira	Prova Régia	
WINERY	WINE NAME	
Arinto	2010	
VARIETY	YEAR	
Bucelas, Portugal	$16	
ORIGIN	PRICE	CLOSURE

While the Quinta da Romeira winery has roots dating back to Portuguese royalty in the 13th century, it started to create its reputation for quality wines in 1703.

The Prova Régia, however, is very new; it was created in 1992. This delicate, dry, fruity white is one for fans of dry Riesling, uncorked Chardonnay and Albarino. It's made from Arinto, a Portuguese grape that, here, is reminiscent of Meyer lemons, those little almost-sweet lemons that smell and taste so delicious.

TRIVIA The Duke of Wellington—who led the army that defeated Napoleon at the Battle of Waterloo in 1815—was a big fan of white wines from Bucelas, and, sort of like rap stars singing about cognac or Moscato today, set off a Portuguese wine craze in England.

PAIR WITH Fresh oysters, mussels, sushi, calamari. Or just enjoy it chilled, by itself on a patio.

UNCORK Brunch, light lunches, with wine geeks and European history buffs.

JANÉ VENTURA

Jané Ventura	15 Vinyes	
WINERY	WINE NAME	
White blend (see below)	2011	
VARIETY	YEAR	
Baix Penedes, Spain	$20	
ORIGIN	PRICE	CLOSURE

Jané (pronounced *Jah-NAY*, with the *J* being a soft *g*) Ventura is a crisp white sipper made from Xarel-lo (pronounced *Shah-REL-lo*; the hyphen is supposed to be in the grape name), Muscat, Sauvignon Blanc and Malvasia de Sitges grapes. The grapes come from 15 vineyards—the reason behind the name 15 Vinyes ("15 Vines" in Spanish). Expect a tasty, citrusy, minerally white wine for hot days and for anyone who likes white wines.

TRIVIA Baix Penedes is famous for its "castellers,"—people who, in an ancient tradition of this region, climb on top of each other to see who can build the tallest human pyramid. Drink enough of this wine and you may want to build a human pyramid yourself.

PAIR WITH Seafood (mussels, scallops, sushi, white fish), charcuterie, goat cheese. Serve chilled.

UNCORK Going fishing, going to the beach, any time you feel like making a human pyramid.

PERFUM DE VI BLANC

Raventós i Blanc	Perfum de Vi Blanc	
WINERY	WINE NAME	
Muscat/Macabeo	2010	
VARIETY	YEAR	
Penèdes, Spain	$23	
ORIGIN	PRICE	CLOSURE

This fresh white wine is made mostly from Muscat grapes (with some indigenous Spanish Macabeo grapes, too). Thanks to the Muscat, it features floral notes—but you aren't going to smell like you lost a catfight with the women at the perfume counter in a department store. Rather, it's crisp and refreshing, slightly green and herbal. It comes from a family that has been making wine on the same land since 1497. Especially renowned for their sparkling wines (alas, too expensive for this book), they also make red and white table wines, such as this lovely example.

TRIVIA Look carefully and you'll see a tiny symbol of an oak tree on this label. It's the winery's symbol, and it stands for the family's strength and commitment to the land. (The tree literally exists, just out front of the winery's main building.)

PAIR WITH White fish, scallops, roast chicken, salads. Serve chilled.

UNCORK On hot summer days, Sunday lunches, dinner with wine geeks.

CHATEAU ST. JEAN

Chateau St. Jean	Sonoma	
WINERY	WINE NAME	
Chardonnay	2010	
VARIETY	YEAR	
Sonoma County, California, US	$20	
ORIGIN	PRICE	CLOSURE

California Chardonnay sometimes gets knocked by know-it-all wine drinkers, who think they don't like the white wine grape, which once pretty much defined white wine in North America. But really, served slightly chilled, Chardonnay is incredibly food friendly and enjoyable. Year after year, Chateau St. Jean makes a reliable California Chardonnay at a very good price. Expect creamy notes of pear, melon, pineapple and citrus. As for the name, "Jean" is pronounced like the "jean" in blue jeans, and the "St." stands for saint. You don't need a French accent, unless you want to pronounce "château" correctly.

TRIVIA The estate's château was built in the 1920s for a rich family from Michigan, who made their money in timber and iron. They planted grapes, but during Prohibition switched to walnuts and prunes. In 1973, Chateau St. Jean was created, and the land once again was planted with grapes.

PAIR WITH Grilled fish, roast chicken or turkey, lobster with butter, creamy white pasta sauces, creamy soups. Very versatile, and it's great by itself, too. Serve chilled.

UNCORK Sunday dinners with your aunties, Thanksgiving, Christmas.

CHATEAU STE. MICHELLE

Chateau Ste. Michelle
WINERY

Riesling — VARIETY
2011 — YEAR

Columbia Valley, US — ORIGIN
$18 — PRICE
CLOSURE

Chateau Ste. Michelle is Washington's oldest winery and, indeed, was the first to establish Washington as a place where wine could even be made. The grand estate would look perfectly at home in Europe, but is in Woodinville, Washington, just over 200 kilometres south of Vancouver, BC.

This semi-dry sipper offers tasty peach-lime-citrus flavours, and it has just enough sweetness to cut through salty dishes.

TRIVIA In Washington, Chateau Ste. Michelle isn't just famous for awesome wines at good prices. Every summer, the winery hosts popular outdoor concerts; past performers include INXS, the Beach Boys and Ringo Starr.

PAIR WITH Ham, Asian takeout (Indian, Vietnamese, Thai, Chinese). Serve chilled.

UNCORK Now, for Friday night takeout, Easter dinner.

RA! RA!
ROSÉ!
(PINK
DRINKS)

ARTAZURI

Bodegas Artadi	Artazuri	
WINERY	WINE NAME	
Grenache	2011	
VARIETY	YEAR	
Navarra, Spain	$18	
ORIGIN	PRICE	CLOSURE

Artazuri comes from renowned winemaker Juan Carlos López de Lacalle. The grapes come from Navarra, a relatively small region in northeastern Spain, where the Running of the Bulls takes place every July. This ancient festival has been going on since the 1600s, and at the end of the run there's a bullfight. It makes the Calgary Stampede look pretty tame. Really.

Made from 100 percent Grenache (*Garnacha*, in Spanish) grapes, this beautiful pink offers plenty of style and taste—raspberry, strawberry, lemon deliciousness. Resist the urge to guzzle it.

TRIVIA Although Ernest Hemingway never actually ran with the bulls, he wrote about it in his book *The Sun Also Rises*. At the time, he was a reporter for the *Toronto Star*.

PAIR WITH Grilled chicken, charcuterie (especially with Serrano, a type of Spanish ham), salads, mild seafood dishes. Serve chilled.

UNCORK While reading Hemingway on a hot summer day, when you wish you were enjoying a hot summer day, picnics, bullfights.

CHATEAU DE LANCYRE

Chateau de Lancyre	Pic Saint-Loup	
WINERY	WINE NAME	
Syrah/Grenache/Cinsault	2010	
VARIETY	YEAR	
Coteaux du Languedoc, France	$19	
ORIGIN	PRICE	CLOSURE

In the 1970s, a couple of families bought this place—built in the 1500s, on the ruins of an ancient fort—then set to fixing it up and, of course, making some wine. Now they're in a hotter-than-hot spot; with the best wines in the Languedoc, Pic Saint-Loup is one of the trendiest places for winemaking in France these days. As for the wine, this one is peachy-pink, fruity and dry, with mineral, pear and berry notes.

TRIVIA Pic Saint-Loup gets its name (which literally translates as "Peak Saint Wolf") from a wolf-tooth-shaped mountain that juts up in the region.

PAIR WITH Charcuterie, kebabs, brandade, hearty salads (niçoise, perhaps), grilled vegetables. Serve chilled.

UNCORK With friends, picnics, weekend lunches.

DOMAINE LAFOND

Domaine Lafond	Roc-Epine	
WINERY	WINE NAME	
Rosé blend (see below)	2011	
VARIETY	YEAR	
Tavel, France	$20	
ORIGIN	PRICE	CLOSURE

A perfect strawberry-red colour, this dry, medium-bodied rosé comes from a small family-owned winery in France. The name Roc-Epine comes from Roquepine, a famous French trotting horse of the 1960s and 1970s. The winery's owner changed the spelling, to try to make the word look more "Provençal." And presto, Domaine Lafond Roc-Epine was born.

As for the grapes? It's a mix—mostly Grenache, plus Cinsault, Syrah, Carignan and a bit of Clairette, Picpoul, Bourboulenc and Mourvèdre. There will be a test on that later. Just kidding. Seriously though, if a wine snob asks, just tell them it's a blend of indigenous French grapes and then tell them to be quiet if they want you to share. Then taste those fruity, herbal, mineral notes.

TRIVIA Tavel—part of the Rhône Valley—has long been famous for its rosés, which have been favourites with kings and popes for generations. The French novelist Honoré de Balzac was also a fan.

PAIR WITH Fresh oysters, scallops, sushi, soft white cheeses, bouillabaisse. Serve chilled.

UNCORK Picnics, patios, Earth Day, mid-week pick-me-ups. One of the only rosé wines that can also be cellared successfully (most are made to drink young).

DOMAINES PIERRE GAILLARD

Domaines Pierre Gaillard	Rosé de Syrah	
WINERY	WINE NAME	
Syrah	2011	
VARIETY	YEAR	
Collines Rhodaniennes, France	$18	
ORIGIN	PRICE	CLOSURE

Pierre Gaillard is another one of those rock stars of the wine world, the kind of guy that inspires awe among cork dorks the world over. He has vineyards in a few spots in France, but the grapes for this one come from a sub-region of the Rhône Valley. You may have guessed by the wine's name that those grapes are Syrah. It's dark watermelon-red in colour and has notes of cherry and melon. Not too much acidity—this one's strong but reserved.

TRIVIA Rosé wine is not a mixture of red and white wines. It's made by crushing red-skinned (sometimes called "black") grapes and removing them from the liquid after a short time, a few hours or up to about three days. The longer the skins stay with the liquid, the more intense the colour will be.

PAIR WITH Charcuterie (fancy cold cuts), goat-cheese tarts, gourmet flatbread pizza. Serve chilled.

UNCORK With wine geeks, summer days, picnics, turkey days, Valentine's Day.

JOSÉ'S ROSÉ

Wine by Joe	José's Rosé	
WINERY	WINE NAME	
Rosé blend (see below)	2010	
VARIETY	YEAR	
Willamette Valley, Oregon, US	$16	
ORIGIN	PRICE	CLOSURE

There really is a guy named Joe here—Joe Dobbes is the winery's owner, hence the rosé's José. Say that 10 times fast. While Dobbes and his team make many more "serious" wines, including a range of wonderful Pinot Noirs, they also realize that wine is also about sharing good times with friends—which is exactly what this rosé is about. Fun, unpretentious, made for drinking now, perhaps on a picnic blanket on a hot day. Made from a blend of mostly Pinot Noir with a bit of Pinot Blanc, Muscat and Syrah tossed in, it's zingy and as pink as a sunrise. Look for flavours of watermelon, strawberries and citrus.

TRIVIA A portion of all Joe Dobbes wine sales go to a charity that works toward suicide prevention. The charity was personally chosen by Dobbes, who lost his older brother to suicide.

PAIR WITH Charcuterie (fancy cold cuts), roast chicken, salads, watermelon. Serve chilled.

UNCORK Picnics, patios, birthday parties, turning every day into a reason for celebration.

NATURE!

Borie de Maurel	Nature!	
WINERY	WINE NAME	
Rosé blend	Non-vintage	
VARIETY	YEAR	
Minervois, Languedoc, France	$17	
ORIGIN	PRICE	CLOSURE

Michel Escande and his wife Sylvie set up shop here in 1989, and now their sons are also working with them and their team. The eldest, Gabriel Escande, created this dark pink rosé—a rosé for red wine fans—for his friends, after noticing they preferred drinking cocktails and beer. He wanted to make a wine that they'd all enjoy. Lucky friends—and lucky us, who are now able to find it, too. It's dry but on the sweeter side of dry. It's not too acidic, and it has candy, watermelon and herbal notes.

TRIVIA The cap for this wine features the words "to drink fresh" in more than 15 languages. I gave up trying to count.

PAIR WITH Charcuterie (fancy cold cuts), pizza margherita, fancy mild cheeses. Serve chilled.

UNCORK Now, with good buddies. Nature! (As creator Gabriel Escande intended.)

PINOT ROSÉ

Bird in Hand
WINERY

Pinot Noir — VARIETY
2010 — YEAR

Adelaide Hills, Australia — ORIGIN
$25 — PRICE
CLOSURE

Bird in Hand is a relatively small, family-owned Australian winery, offering a range of eight wines, including this lovely, fruity rosé. What makes it so great? It's a bird with balls. Literally (see Trivia note). I mean it has lots of body, of course. Considering it's a rosé—not exactly a wine renowned for being big—it packs a wallop of fruity wonderfulness.

And it comes from Adelaide Hills. Truly one of the most beautiful wine regions in the world, Adelaide Hills is so green and lush, with so many excellent little shops, restaurants and wineries, it feels like paradise for wine lovers.

TRIVIA Know anyone who's a Wimbledon fan? Since 2007, this wine has been the famous tennis tournament's official wine.

PAIR WITH Charcuterie (fancy cold cuts), strawberries and cream (like they do at Wimbledon), seafood. Serve chilled.

UNCORK Hot afternoons on the patio, wearing crazy hats while watching Wimbledon, post-tennis recovery.

QUAILS' GATE

Quails' Gate
WINERY

Rosé blend (see below) | 2011
VARIETY | YEAR

Okanagan Valley, BC, Canada | $15
ORIGIN | PRICE | CLOSURE

The family behind Quails' Gate has been in the Okanagan Valley since 1908, and they planted their first vineyards in 1961—an incredibly long time by Canadian winery standards. Since then, they've won lots of awards and made plenty of vino-loving friends with a full range of wines—including this bright, zingy summer sipper, made from a blend of Gamay Noir, Pinot Noir and Pinot Gris. It'll make you think of a big juicy grapefruit, with a light sprinkle of cinnamon sugar on top. It'll make your mouth water. It'll make you want more.

TRIVIA US president Barack Obama drank Quails' Gate wine on his first trip to Canada, and so did Prince William and Kate Middleton when they were here in 2011.

PAIR WITH Salads, light appetizers, scallops, ginger beef. Serve chilled.

UNCORK As an aperitif, patio days, baby showers.

WHISPERING ANGEL

Caves du Château d'Esclans	Whispering Angel	
WINERY	WINE NAME	
Rosé blend	2011	
VARIETY	YEAR	
Côtes de Provence, France	$22	
ORIGIN	PRICE	CLOSURE

There are two main men behind the wines at Caves du Château d'Esclans—one Sacha Lichine, the owner, and Patrick Leon, the oenologist aka winemaker. I'm not one to name-drop (well, just a little), but Lichine's father, Alexis, was a famous wine writer and owner of a winery called Château Prieuré-Lichine in Bordeaux. Sacha's an over-achiever in his own life—he became an internationally renowned negociant (a sort of wine importer/negotiator) before he turned 30. And Leon worked at a few of the world's greatest wineries—Opus One, Clerc Milon, Mouton Rothschild—before pairing up with Lichine to make top-notch rosé. Yes, rosé. The world's best. Now you know why you have to find a bottle of this one. By the way, it's pale pink and dry, with delicate fruity notes.

TRIVIA When asked how to learn more about wine, Sacha's father apparently had a few good words of advice. "Buy a corkscrew and use it," he'd say. Sacha obviously listened.

PAIR WITH Drink by itself. But if you must share it with food, try salmon, soft cheeses, sushi. Serve chilled.

UNCORK With people you love, wine geeks, me.

BARGAIN
BUBBLES

ADAMI

Adriano Adami	Garbèl	
WINERY	WINE NAME	
Prosecco	Non-vintage	
TYPE	YEAR	
Treviso, Veneto, Italy	$21	
ORIGIN	PRICE	CLOSURE

By international law, Prosecco can only be made in Italy's Veneto region. This Prosecco comes from the Adami winemaking family near the city of Treviso, just northwest of Venice. They've been growing grapes and making Prosecco on this land since 1920, and by 1933 they were already winning awards for their fine bubbles.

This bubbly treat features a fancy silk label and very pleasant notes of citrus, apple and pear.

TRIVIA The word *garbèl* refers to a crisp, dry, slightly tart wine in one of the region's ancient local dialects.

PAIR WITH Sushi, soft cheeses. Or drink by itself, as it makes a wonderful aperitif. Drink it now, slightly chilled. Don't try to cellar Prosecco, any Prosecco, as it's made to enjoy while it's young and fresh. Serve chilled.

UNCORK Friday nights, Saturday nights, Sundays, Mondays, Wednesdays (of course), and we can't forget Tuesdays or Thursdays.

ANTECH

Antech
WINERY

Blanquette de Limoux — 2011
TYPE — YEAR

Limoux, France — $22
ORIGIN — PRICE — CLOSURE

This wine appeared in the 2010 edition of *Uncorked!* The equivalent of a heartbreakingly good chanteuse busking on a Parisian street corner, this relatively uncommon but beautiful sparkler deserves to be a star. If ever a wine was elegant, it would be this creamy, flowery Blanquette from France's Languedoc region. (Limoux is a subregion.) Pronounced *Ann-TESH*, it's made mostly from a grape called Mauzac Blanc (also known as Blanquette, which means "white" in Occitan, the region's own language). It's dry, with notes of lemon, honey and brioche, with mild bubbles for those who don't like too much fizz in their fizz.

TRIVIA Languedoc locals believe that ancient monks created the world's first sparkling wine in this region in the early 1500s—long before champagne burst onto the bubble scene.

PAIR WITH Fresh oysters, sushi. Or just drink by itself. Serve chilled.

UNCORK Any time, any day of the week, any special occasion.

COLLALTO

Collalto	Conegliano e Valdobbiadene Extra Dry	
WINERY	WINE NAME	
Prosecco	Non-vintage	
TYPE	YEAR	
Veneto, Italy	$21	
ORIGIN	PRICE	CLOSURE

I've served this refreshing sparkler a couple of times at parties, and every time, people go crazy for it. It's made from 100 percent Glera grapes, an ancient indigenous white Italian variety that's primarily used in Prosecco. It features fruity notes of citrus and pear, and it's made using the charmat method, which means it develops its bubbles in stainless steel tanks, not in the bottle (a way that wine folk like to call *méthode champenoise* or "traditional method").

Winemaker Isabella Collalto oversees an estate that has been in her family for more than 1,000 years; perhaps not surprisingly, all of her grapes are estate grown.

TRIVIA The Veneto region includes two of Italy's most famous cities, Venice (canals and gondolas) and Verona (where Shakespeare's Romeo and Juliet lived out their short, star-crossed lives).

PAIR WITH Brunch dishes, sushi, calamari, or just enjoy by itself. Serve chilled.

UNCORK Mother's Day, brunch gatherings, Grandma's birthday, any day you need/want/need bubbles.

DR. L SPARKLING RIESLING

Loosen Bros.	Dr. L Sparkling Riesling	
WINERY	WINE NAME	
Riesling	2011	
TYPE	YEAR	
Mosel, Germany	$17	
ORIGIN	PRICE	CLOSURE

An apple a day may keep the doctor away, but when the doctor is this much fun, you'll want him to stick around. The Loosen family has been making wine for more than 200 years, and the winery is still family owned—rare, in these days of major corporations and multinationals. Two brothers, Ernst and Thomas Loosen, currently head up the winery and its various projects.

The Dr. L Sparkling Riesling offers off-dry, slightly steely notes of citrus and a hint of ginger and juicy apples. Yes, apples.

TRIVIA Sparkling wine has been made for generations in Germany—where it is often called *sekt*.

PAIR WITH Sushi, light aperitifs. Serve chilled.

UNCORK Any time there's a doctor in the house, parties with PhD candidates, weddings, parties, anything.

FLOR

Flor

WINERY

Prosecco	Non-vintage	
TYPE	YEAR	
Valdobbiadene, Italy	$21	
ORIGIN	PRICE	CLOSURE

Celeb chef groupies may be interested in knowing these elegant bubbles are the result of a joint project between the legendary Mario Batali—the celebrity chef with the expansive girth and the bright orange clogs—and his restaurant partners Lidia Bastianich and her son Joseph. In fact, Flor was created specifically for their restaurants.

Wine snobs will probably just be content to know that the wine inside the bottle is tasty, with zippy acidity and notes of apple, pear, almond and citrus.

TRIVIA Lidia Bastianich is a hotshot chef in her own right, and the author of many cookbooks. As for Batali, he and REM singer Michael Stipe have been friends since they were kids.

PAIR WITH Smoked salmon, seafood appetizers. Or drink by itself. Serve chilled.

UNCORK Now, any time you want to entertain in style, any time you simply want a delicious sparkling wine.

LA MARCA

La Marca

WINERY

Prosecco — TYPE

Non-vintage — YEAR

Treviso, Veneto, Italy — ORIGIN

$20 — PRICE

CLOSURE

Good packaging doesn't always mean good wine, but really, these bargain bubbles are both—a fancy-looking label and a fancy taste, too. They're fresh and clean-tasting, with notes of honey, grapefruit and just a touch of toast.

Created more than 40 years ago, the winery gets its name from La Marca Trevigiana, the heart of Italy's Prosecco region. La Marca's Fabrizio Gatto began his winemaking career at the age of 14 (yes, you read that correctly) when he was accepted into the Conegliano Veneto School of Enology.

TRIVIA More than just stylish wine comes from Treviso; the clothing company Benetton was also founded in the northern Italian city.

PAIR WITH Seafood in garlic butter, salads, sushi, white fish dishes. Or just enjoy it as an aperitif. Serve chilled.

UNCORK Any time, any place, especially if I'm coming for dinner.

PARÉS BALTÀ

Parés Baltà	Brut
WINERY	WINE NAME
Organic cava	Non-vintage
TYPE	YEAR
Penedès, Spain	$20
ORIGIN	PRICE

CLOSURE

This wine appeared in the 2010 edition of *Uncorked!* This family-owned winery is the kind of winery that reminds you that vineyards are about farming. A herd of sheep wander through the vineyards, providing natural fertilization (I'll spare you the graphic details here). And beehives help in pollination. Real farming, real life and real organic winemaking in action. Really good wine, too. Made in the traditional method, this fresh and sophisticated sparkler has creamy, toasty, honey, apple notes. Hard to resist.

TRIVIA Parés Baltà has roots in the winemaking business dating back to 1790. These days, it's managed by two brothers, whose two wives are the winemakers.

PAIR WITH Fresh oysters, shrimp, scallops, fresh fruit in season, Chinese food. Or just enjoy by itself. Serve chilled.

UNCORK Earth Day, Earth Hour, every day.

ROLET

Domaine Rolet, Père et Fils	Rosé Brut	
WINERY	WINE NAME	
Crémant du Jura	Non-vintage	
TYPE	YEAR	
Arbois, Jura, France	$25	
ORIGIN	PRICE	CLOSURE

Perched between Burgundy, France, and Switzerland, Jura is a bit off the beaten track, but it is also where some rather interesting wines are made. This winery, Domaine Rolet—the second-largest in the region—dates back to the 1940s and is still family owned and operated. The family makes a range of wines, including these delicate, dry aromatic peachy-pink–hued bubbles, which are made from a grape called Poulsard, plus Chardonnay and Pinot Noir. Expect hints of cherry, lemon and minerals.

TRIVIA These beautiful bubbles are made in the traditional method—the same way that real champagne is made. It's more expensive, but the resulting wine has smaller bubbles (a good thing, say the critics) and is more complex (also a good thing, say the critics).

PAIR WITH Sushi, roast turkey or chicken, coquilles St. Jacques, Comté cheese. Serve chilled.

UNCORK As an aperitif, on casual Friday nights, Sunday mornings, Grandma's birthday, bridal showers, weddings, New Year's Eve, turkey days.

SEGURA VIUDAS

Segura Viudas	Brut Reserva	
WINERY	WINE NAME	
Cava	Non-vintage	
TYPE	YEAR	
Penèdes, Spain	$16	
ORIGIN	PRICE	CLOSURE

This wine appeared in the 2010 edition of *Uncorked!* Classic bubbles, year after year, at a very, very good price. Real champagne is pricey, but this cava is made following the traditional method used to make champagne and it costs a lot less. *Cava* is the official Spanish word for sparkling wine made in Spain—only in Spain. This dry (brut on the label means it's dry) sparkler is all apples and lime and cream soda; it's a blend of three traditional Spanish cava grapes, Macabeo, Parellada, and Xarel-lo (pronounced *Shah-REL-lo*; yes, that odd little hyphen in the grape name is intentional).

TRIVIA The people behind Segura Viudas began to market their wines internationally in 1969, the same year that Neil Armstrong landed on the moon, Woodstock took place on a farm in New York State and, in Canada, actor and funny guy Rick Mercer was born.

PAIR WITH Tempura, ceviche, fresh oysters, smoked salmon, crab cakes, sushi. Serve chilled.

UNCORK Now, on New Year's Eve, for weddings, baby showers, birthdays, when your favourite team wins.

VEUVE DU VERNAY

Veuve du Vernay	Brut	
WINERY	WINE NAME	
Sparkling white blend (see below)	Non-vintage	
TYPE	YEAR	
Bordeaux, France	$14	
ORIGIN	PRICE	CLOSURE

From Bordeaux, this Veuve du Vernay is a blend of white grapes (Chardonnay, Colombard and Sauvignon Blanc) and it has fresh, fruity notes of lemon meringue, pear and flowers. While the word *brut* literally means "dry" in French, this one is just right. Not too dry, but not sweet, either. It's a sparkling wine from France, but it can't be called champagne because it isn't made in the right region. That's why it says *vin mousseux*, instead of champagne, on the label. That's also why it costs $14 a bottle instead of $60 or much more. Save your cash for other things, like trips to France.

TRIVIA Wines have been made in Bordeaux for more than 2,000 years. More than 80 percent of Bordeaux wines are red and more than 700 million bottles are produced in the region every year.

PAIR WITH Sushi, smoked salmon appetizers, white fish dishes, simple fruit-based desserts. Serve chilled.

UNCORK Now, anniversaries, Valentine's Day, book club, Sunday mornings, Saturday mornings, Friday nights, Wednesday nights, Christmas, New Year's Eve, birthdays, just because you want bubbles.

VILLA TERESA ROSÉ VENETO

Villa Teresa	Rosé Veneto Vino Frizzante	
WINERY	WINE NAME	
Organic sparkling rosé	Non-vintage	
TYPE	YEAR	
Veneto, Italy	$16	
ORIGIN	PRICE	CLOSURE

Made from grapes grown on the banks of Italy's Piave River, this little honey of a wine is just the sort of bubbles you want when you need to cheer up or celebrate. It comes from a family-owned winery in the heart of the Veneto region of Italy—close to Venice and home to Prosecco. But, by law, this sparkler isn't allowed to be called Prosecco because it's a rosé and made from the wrong type of grapes. Still, it has a beautiful dark salmon-pink colour and it's a beautiful package, with an unusual old-fashioned, resealable flip-top closure. Taste this wine and you'll get a mouthful of very fine bubbles with notes of apple, candy, sweet cherry and violet.

TRIVIA This wine is made from Raboso grapes, a red wine grape that's mostly found in Italy's Veneto region, and where researchers believe it likely originated. It's mostly made into sparkling wines such as this one.

PAIR WITH Charcuterie (fancy cold cuts), white fish dishes, sushi. Or just enjoy as an aperitif. Serve chilled.

UNCORK Baby showers, book clubs, brunch, casual Fridays, fashion shows.

SWEET & FORTIFIED WINES

CROFT PINK

Croft	Pink	
WINERY	WINE NAME	
Port	Non-vintage	
TYPE	YEAR	
Douro Valley, Portugal	$24	
ORIGIN	PRICE	CLOSURE

Now you can see the world through rose-coloured glasses—glasses of pink port, that is. Indeed, this may be the most unconventional port you and I ever try.

But the creators are the real deal, and Croft Pink is definitely a port, from one of Portugal's original port houses. Croft's roots in the business date back to the 1500s.

While most aficionados probably think of port as something to enjoy on a cold winter night, the makers of this rose-coloured fortified wine aim to change that perception. The company's current head describes the new pink wine as "port without rules." Vintage port fans may take some convincing to try this, but it will find fans among those who love sweetish wines and fun cocktails.

TRIVIA The Douro Valley, where port is made, is a UNESCO World Heritage Site. While the area is famous for its port, it produces just as much (often good) table wine.

PAIR WITH Raspberry or strawberry sorbet, vanilla ice cream. For a simple cocktail, add some to Prosecco (one-third Croft Pink, two-thirds Prosecco) or a shot of club soda. Turn it into a slushie drink, or find other cocktail suggestions at croftpink.com.

UNCORK Dessert nights, stagettes, hot summer nights.

DOW'S

Dow's	Late-Bottled Vintage Port	
WINERY	WINE NAME	
Port	2006	
TYPE	YEAR	
Douro, Portugal	$25	
ORIGIN	PRICE	CLOSURE

Dow's—one of the world's great port houses—has been owned by the same family for more than 200 years.

Whatever the house, vintage port is only made in certain "declared" years, years when growing conditions are outstanding. And in other years? That's when we bargain hunters get Late-Bottled Vintage Port, aka LBV Port by those in the know. This LBV Port is delicious, sweet, fruity and rich—a smooth, dark red treat on a cold winter night.

Incidentally, LBV Port has been filtered, so you don't need to decant it, unless you want to feel like an old-fashioned English gentleman.

TRIVIA No one quite knows how port came to be, but legend has it that in the 1700s, wine merchants threw brandy into their wine to stabilize it as it was shipped across the ocean to England. The alcohol in the brandy stops the winemaking process early, when the wine is still fruity and sweet.

PAIR WITH Hard aged cheddar, aged gouda, dark chocolate.

UNCORK Now, winter nights, fall nights, spring nights, summer camping Alberta-style. It won't age as long or as well as vintage port, but you can also put a bottle away for a few years.

ESSENSIA

Quady Winery WINERY	Essensia WINE NAME	
Dessert wine TYPE	2010 YEAR	
California, US ORIGIN	$14 for 375 mL PRICE	CLOSURE

This wine appeared in the 2010 edition of *Uncorked!* Made from Muscat grapes, this wine is a perennial winner because it's pretty (a lovely orange colour) and it smells good (aromas of orange blossoms, honey, apricot, vanilla) and tastes good (notes of tangerines and honey). Sweet but not too, too sweet.

Andrew and Laurel Quady—the couple who started the winery—recommend trying a shot of Essensia with sparkling wine to make an Essensia Royale. Try a few of those with fresh scones and seasonal fruit at your next brunch. No one will remember that you forgot to dust the lampshades.

TRIVIA Andrew Quady worked in pyrotechnics (yeah, fireworks) and munitions before starting up Quady Winery in the 1970s.

PAIR WITH Angel food cake, plain pound cake with whipped cream, flan. Or serve little glasses of it solo. Serve chilled.

UNCORK Brunches, Granny's birthday, bridal showers, birthday parties.

FIELD STONE

Field Stone Fruit Wines	Saskatoon Berry Dessert Wine	
WINERY	WINE NAME	
Dessert wine	Non-vintage	
TYPE	YEAR	
Strathmore, Alberta	$20 for 375 mL	
ORIGIN	PRICE	CLOSURE

This wine appeared in the 2010 edition of *Uncorked!* Alberta has wineries. Fruit wineries, that is. This one, Field Stone, was started in 2005 and is located about half an hour east of Calgary. Stop in for a tour if you're around on a summer weekend. The family-owned operation makes several dessert wines and table wines, mostly from locally grown fruit. If saskatoons aren't your favourite, consider some of the winery's other offerings—blackcurrant, strawberry-rhubarb, wild black cherry and more. Want a quick cocktail? Add a sparkling wine to a bit of this fortified dessert wine for a locavore kir royale—a Canuck take on the classic French drink. (The word "fortified" means it has had distilled alcohol, aka brandy added to it.) While not technically organic, Field Stone's wines are made without pesticides or fungicides.

TRIVIA Saskatoons are little berries that look a bit like blueberries but have their own distinctive taste. Unlike blueberries, they thrive in Alberta, despite our unpredictable weather. Bears love their taste.

PAIR WITH Homemade vanilla ice cream, plain cheesecake, angel food cake and whipped cream. Or serve solo. Serve chilled.

UNCORK For locavore dinners, 100-mile diets, bridal showers, weddings, Sunday evening desserts in winter, any time you need a pretty dessert wine and you're feeling too broke to buy icewine.

FONSECA PORTO BIN NO. 27

Fonseca	Bin No. 27 Finest Reserve	
WINERY	WINE NAME	
Port	Non-vintage	
TYPE	YEAR	
Douro Valley, Portugal	$22	
ORIGIN	PRICE	CLOSURE

This wine appeared in the 2010 edition of *Uncorked!* If you like big, jammy, full-bodied red wines, you should try port. Port wines are fortified, meaning that hard alcohol (spirits) is added to the wine to stop the fermentation process, the process that normally turns all that juice into what we know as wine. A fortified wine can't have the word "port" on the label unless it comes from Portugal's Douro Valley, home to the real deal. This ruby port, a sweet beauty of a wine, has lots of rich dark fruit and cherry notes, and is ready to drink now. A great introduction to the world of port and fortified wines. In case you're worried, you don't need to decant this one.

TRIVIA Bin 27 was the vat closest to the house of the late Fonseca port winemaker Bruce Guimaraens. When he went to fetch a decanter of "house port," it was from Bin 27. The family's house port wasn't released commercially until 1972.

PAIR WITH Blue cheese (especially Cambozola or Gorgonzola), dark chocolate mousse, aged gouda, flan, crème caramel. Or drink by itself. Chill slightly (a little cooler than room temperature).

UNCORK Now, for the first snowfall of the year, January cold spells, spring snowfalls.

HARVEY'S BRISTOL CREAM

Harvey's	Bristol Cream	
WINERY	WINE NAME	
Sherry	Non-vintage	
TYPE	YEAR	
Jerez, Spain	$16	
ORIGIN	PRICE	CLOSURE

Rich. Sweet. Nutty. Slightly citrusy. Creamy. Smooth. And very, very different from what most of us think of as wine. But it's worth seeking out, if only to truly understand the world of wine history. Harvey's Bristol Cream was the world's first cream sherry. It was invented by John and Edward Harvey in the late 1800s in Bristol, England, hence the name. Their father, John senior, was a wine merchant who started the sherry business in 1796.

TRIVIA The word "sherry" is likely an English adaptation of *Jerez*, the name of the town in southern Spain in which sherry originated. *Jerez* in turn likely comes from *Sherish*, the Arabic name for the town—Jerez dates back to the days of the Moors.

PAIR WITH Vanilla ice cream, baklava. Or enjoy by itself on ice.

UNCORK With history buffs, Grandma and wine geeks.

LILLET

Lillet
WINERY

Aperitif
TYPE

Non-vintage
YEAR

Bordeaux, France
ORIGIN

$18
PRICE

CLOSURE

This French aperitif wine has been around since the late 1800s, and it was especially big in the 1920s. It's made from a combination of white wines (Sauvignon Blanc, Sémillon and Muscadelle), citrus liqueurs and a type of Peruvian tree bark that contains quinine.

Don't let that scare you off trying this unusual—at least to North Americans—wine. It's slightly sweet but not overwhelmingly so; you'll get notes of honey, candied orange and flowers if you taste it. It's also sometimes referred to as Lillet Blanc, because there's a red version, too.

TRIVIA James Bond called for Lillet in *Casino Royale*, asking for a dry martini . . . with "half a measure" of Lillet.

PAIR WITH An ice cube and a thin slice of orange or lemon. Or add cocktail ingredients—everything from gin to orange juice.

UNCORK As an aperitif, with Francophiles, at Roaring '20s-themed parties, James Bond fan club meetings. Serve chilled.

LUSTAU EAST INDIA SOLERA

Emilio Lustau
WINERY

Sherry
TYPE

Non-vintage
YEAR

Jerez, Spain
ORIGIN

$18 for 375 mL
PRICE

CLOSURE

This wine appeared in the 2010 edition of *Uncorked!* Sherry is one of the world's oldest and greatest wines, and every wine lover should try it at least once. If legwarmers, Smurfs and the Three Stooges can come back in style, then sherry should have its day in the sun again, too. Here's to being at the vanguard of a new trend.

This sherry smells like raisins, dried figs, nuts, candied orange peel and Christmas fruitcake. Unlike fruitcake, I don't want to give it away as soon as someone gives it to me.

TRIVIA The solera process was invented to even out quality between vintage years (you'll notice this bottle doesn't have a specific year on it). Every year, a little wine is removed (and bottled) from the oldest barrels and replaced with wine from the next-oldest barrels, and so on.

PAIR WITH Chocolate, cheese, crème brûlée, Christmas pudding. Or serve solo at the end of a meal.

UNCORK Fancy dinner parties, the first snowfall of the season, dinner with Grandma. Or with wine geeks and steampunk fans (who will love the packaging).

NIVOLE

Michele Chiarlo	Nivole Moscato d'Asti	
WINERY	WINE NAME	
Sweet sparkling dessert wine	2010	
TYPE	YEAR	
Calamandrana, Italy	$16 for 375 mL	
ORIGIN	PRICE	CLOSURE

Moscato is one of the hottest wine trends in North America these days, so why not track down a fine example from the country that created the original? While Moscato can be made anywhere, Moscato d'Asti can only be made in Italy's Piedmont region.

This delicate, fresh wine is low in alcohol (5 percent) and gently sweet, with delicious fruity notes and fine bubbles. (Don't expect this to have the bubbles that, say, champagne does; these are soft, almost more frothy than bubbly.) While Michele Chiarlo and his team have created their reputation for phenomenal reds, this one is a delicate, pretty charmer.

TRIVIA Sales of Moscato wines amounted to more than $300 million in the US in 2011.

PAIR WITH Fresh fruit, flan, pound cake.

UNCORK Now, Grandma's birthday, desserts, picnics. Serve chilled.

OJALESHI

Tbilvino	Ojaleshi	
WINERY	WINE NAME	
Semi-sweet red wine	2011	
TYPE	YEAR	
Lechkhumi/Samegrelo, Georgia	$18	
ORIGIN	PRICE	CLOSURE

One of the world's most ancient wine regions, Georgia boasts historical evidence of winemaking that dates back more than 8,000 years. Formerly part of the Soviet Union, the Republic of Georgia is now an independent country—and we are getting a chance to try its wines. This one—made from the Ojaleshi grape, an indigenous Georgian grape, is wildly different from anything we in North America typically think of as wine. It is earthy, spicy, somewhat sweet, sort of like port but different, sort of like a big jammy red but different.

The winery, Tbilvino, is a large family-owned winery. The very modern winemaking facilities are located in Tbilisi, the country's capital and largest city, but its vineyards are scattered around the country.

TRIVIA In Georgia, instead of saying "Cheers," people say, "Gagimarjos!" (I've spelled it phonetically as the Georgian alphabet is different than ours.) The word literally translates as "Be triumphant!"

PAIR WITH Nuts (especially walnuts), hard cheeses. Or just enjoy by itself.

UNCORK Before battles, after turkey dinners, cold winter nights.

OTIMA 10

Warre's	Otima 10-Year-Old Tawny	
WINERY	WINE NAME	
Port	Non-vintage	
TYPE	YEAR	
Douro Valley, Portugal	$23 for 500 mL	
ORIGIN	PRICE	CLOSURE

Tawny port is made when red wine is aged for a long time in wooden barrels. That time in wood oxidizes the wine, concentrates its flavour and softens its colour.

I generally like port's old-fashioned packaging—dark bottles, the swirly fonts on black-and-white labels—but I love this modern clear glass bottle, too, which makes a fashion statement even before you try the fortified wine inside. Otima 10 is just what you'd expect a tawny port to be—a gorgeous rich red-brown, with mellow notes of caramel candies, orange, dried apricot and gingerbread spices.

TRIVIA The Symington family—which owns Warre's—has been in the port business for 13 generations, more than 350 years. Now, that's a family business.

PAIR WITH Chocolate, pecan pie. Or just enjoy by itself.

UNCORK Dinners with friends, camping trips, turkey dinners, any time you have friends over but don't have time to make dessert. Serve slightly chilled.

ZAGARA

Marchesi di Barolo	Zagara Moscato d'Asti	
WINERY	WINE NAME	
Sweet sparkling dessert wine	2011	
TYPE	YEAR	
Piedmont, Italy	$19	
ORIGIN	PRICE	CLOSURE

This wine appeared in the 2010 edition of *Uncorked!* What a difference a couple of years can make in the world of wine trends. Since the first book was published in 2010, Moscato has become North America's trendiest wine. And why not? It's sweet. It's fizzy. It tastes good. And it's low in alcohol, so you can drink this without getting slammed—well, without getting slammed quickly.

Perhaps not surprising, considering the winery's name, Marchesi di Barolo is famous for its Barolo. These legendary Italian reds—made from the Nebbiolo grape—age forever and cost a lot. Luckily for us, Marchesi di Barolo also makes this fun sipper, so we can enjoy the winery's offerings even if we can't afford the famous stuff.

TRIVIA Speaking of famous, North American rap and hip-hop stars likely started the Moscato trend. Kanye West has served it at his parties. And Li'l Kim and Canuck rapper Drake have both sung about it.

PAIR WITH Fresh fruit, pound cake, crème brûlée, pannacotta. Or just drink it chilled, with a side order of hip-hop tunes.

UNCORK Now, at parties, Mother's Day, brunch, bridal showers, desserts with Italophiles. Serve chilled.

TEN AWESOME WINES THAT COST MORE THAN $25 BUT LESS THAN $50

Ready to splurge? Don't mind spending slightly more than $25? Here are 10 wines worth checking out.

1. Joseph Burrier, Château de Beauregard, Colonies de Rochegrès, Fleurie, 2009 (Fleurie, Burgundy, France) **$30**
2. Botani, Moscatel Seco, 2011 (Sierras de Malaga, Spain) **$26**
3. Michael David Winery, 6th Sense Syrah, 2010 (Lodi, California, US) **$26**
4. Clos du Val, Cabernet Sauvignon, 2009 (Napa Valley, California, US) **$37**
5. Plume, Cabernet Sauvignon, 2009 (Napa Valley, California, US) **$29**
6. Greenstone Vineyards, Shiraz, 2009 (Heathcote, Australia) **$33**
7. Tolaini Wines, Valdisanti, 2008 (Tuscany, Italy) **$45**
8. JoieFarm, PTG, 2009 (Okanagan Valley, BC, Canada) **$35**
9. Evening Land Vineyards, Blue Label Pinot Noir, 2009 (Oregon, US) **$35**
10. Osoyoos Larose, Pétales d'Osoyoos, 2009 (Okanagan Valley, BC, Canada) **$35**

WHERE TO BUY THESE WINES

Many of these wines are available at wine shops across the province. If you're looking for a particular label, however, and you can't find it, try the following:

GO TO ALBERTA-LIQUORCONNECT.COM.

This site is run by the Alberta government and you can search to find the name of the importer, and, in most cases, individual stores that carry or have carried the product. Call to ensure stock before you show up and demand a case.

CHECK OUT SOME OF THE ONLINE SHOPPING SITES.

At least two, zyn.ca (403-543-8900) and Kensington Wine Market (1-888-283-9004), can ship wines across the province. Others, such as highlanderwine.com (1-403-777-1922) can ship within Calgary. Alberta Winestein is a new online retailer that aims to bring together small independent wine shops, wineries and even gourmet food vendors with customers across Alberta. You can order online and have the wines delivered to your door. Go to albertawinestein.com for information.

GO TO EVERYTHINGWINE.CA FOR INFORMATION.

Everything Wine—an online wine shop based in British Columbia—will soon be expanding to Alberta.

FURTHER RESOURCES

READ A BOOK

Want to know more about wine? There are dozens of great books out there that will inspire you and further your wine knowledge. Here are a few of my favourites.

1,000 Great Everyday Wines from the World's Best Wineries, edited by Jim Gordon (Dorling Kindersley)

Any of the Dummies guides for wine lovers, especially the ones by Ed McCarthy, including *Wine for Dummies* and *Red Wine for Dummies* (John Wiley and Sons)

Discovering Wine: A Refreshingly Unfussy Beginner's Guide to Finding, Tasting, Judging, Storing, Serving, Cellaring and, Most of All, Discovering Wine, by Joanna Simon (Simon & Schuster)

Kevin Zraly's Windows on the World Complete Wine Course (Sterling Publishing)

The Oxford Companion to Wine, edited by Jancis Robinson (Oxford University Press)

Tony Aspler's Cellar Book: How to Design, Build, Stock and Manage Your Wine Cellar Wherever You Live (Random House Canada)

Wine: An Introduction, by Joanna Simon (Dorling Kindersley)

The World Atlas of Wine, by Hugh Johnson and Jancis Robinson (Mitchell Beazley)

TAKE A CLASS

Most large wine stores offer tastings and seminars, or ask the sommeliers at your favourite local restaurants if they host winemakers' dinners.

Or check out a wine organization:

- The Wine & Spirit Education Trust (WSET, wset.co.uk) offers courses around the world, including in Calgary, and if you pass the exam at the end you'll achieve international certification—handy, in case you ever need to impress, oh, say, a cute single person at a wine bar on the other side of the world. See finevintageltd.com for details on the course in Canadian cities.

- The International Sommelier Guilde (www.internationalsommelier.com) is another globally recognized certificate program. Like WSET, there are different levels. Take just one, or work your way to the top.

- The European Wine Academy (europeanwineacademy.org) offers courses in English for beginners, professionals and wannabe professionals. Some of the courses are offered online, so it doesn't matter where you live.

- The French Wine Society (frenchwinesociety.org) offers courses across North America and in France, including various offerings at Metrovino in Calgary. Or you can sign up to take online courses or a tour.

ACKNOWLEDGEMENTS

THANK YOU—

To Anders, Erik and Steen, who put up with me and a houseful of bottles. To my parents, Phil and Phyllis, who started me on this crazy, wine-soaked journey, and who have always shared their favourite deals (and found time to take care of two rascally grandkids so I could meet deadlines). To all my aunts and uncles and cousins who bought the last book and told all of their friends—I love you! To my brother, Doug, and to Shirley, Mike and Annette, Hildur and Alex, Alison and Don, Donna, Val and Robert, Chris and Leonie, Harry and Dianne, Kevin and Gordon, Aviv and Michal, Kevin and Mairi, for dinners, wine and endless conversations about wine. To my friends in the wine industry in Canada and beyond, for so generously sharing samples and suggestions, and for answering my never-ending questions. To my friends and colleagues at the *Calgary Herald* and *Wine Access*, especially Darren, Tom, Tony and Val B. for your patience, editing skills and tasting tips. To the folks at CBC Radio, especially Russell Bowers. And to the wonderful folks at Whitecap, for making the second book as much fun as the first.

INDEX

Want to know how to use this index? Look for wines under the winery name (this is followed by the specific wine name, if there is any, for example, Jané Ventura '15 Vinyes').

Also look for wines under a grape category ("Cabernet Sauvignon", for example) or wine type ("sparkling wine", for example), or under "red blends", "white blends" or "organic wines". If you're looking for wines from a specific country or region, go back to the table of contents at the front of the book and go to the region you're interested in from there. Can't find what you're looking for? Bust out and try something new. You may be pleasantly surprised.

A

B

C

D

E

F

G

H

J

K

L

M

N

O

P

Q

R

S

T

V

W

Z

ABOUT THE AUTHOR

Photo by Jared Sych

Born and raised in Alberta, Shelley Boettcher once had a psychic tell her she'd make a good used-car salesman. Instead, she became a writer after stints as a cook, a chambermaid, a nanny and the only woman on a rural construction crew.

Based in Calgary, she is an award-winning writer whose work has appeared in newspapers and magazines around the world. These days, she is the executive editor of *Wine Access*, a national wine magazine, and she's the wine columnist for the *Calgary Herald*.

She holds a master's degree in journalism from the University of Western Ontario, and intermediate certification from the Wine and Spirits Education Trust.

Follow her on Twitter @shelley_wine, and become a friend of the book on Facebook by searching "Uncorked." She also blogs at www.shelleyboettcher.com.